ST. LOUIS
COFFEE

ST. LOUIS COFFEE

A Stimulating History

DEBORAH REINHARDT

AMERICAN PALATE

Published by American Palate
A division of The History Press
Charleston, SC
www.historypress.com

Front cover, top: Wasif Malik via Flickr; *bottom*: Vivian Evans via Flickr.
Back cover: Missouri Historical Society, St. Louis.

First published 2022

Manufactured in the United States

ISBN 9781467152327

Library of Congress Control Number: 2022943535

Notice: The information in this book is true and complete to the best of our knowledge. It is offered without guarantee on the part of the author or The History Press. The author and The History Press disclaim all liability in connection with the use of this book.

I dedicate this book to the memory of my parents, Catherine and Robert Reinhardt, and to my paternal grandparents, Dorothy and Lares Reinhardt. In their home, the coffee pot was always on and ready to share with friends or family. I'm forever grateful to them for modeling true hospitality.

CONTENTS

PREFACE

Coffee and my family are intertwined. My great-grandfather Frederick Reinhardt weighed coffee. Growing up in St. Louis, I was lucky enough to live with my parents and grandparents, and the coffee pot was always on, because one never knew who might be dropping by for a visit.

Whether it was one of my uncles, neighbors or even Red, our milkman, seated at her table, my grandmother Dorothy Reinhardt always had a fresh cup of java to offer them, along with a slice of her delicious coffee cake. When we moved into another house, my mother, Catherine (Katie) Reinhardt, poured many cups for new friends.

What made this special were the conversations around the kitchen table my family engaged in while holding their warm mugs of coffee. Convivial and spirited talk flowed from our kitchen. What I don't remember are harsh words, because back then a coffee klatsch was supposed to be warm and welcoming, just like the dark liquid in the cups.

Naturally, I grew up drinking coffee. As a child, my "coffee" was a cup of milk with a teaspoon of Mom's coffee stirred in, but at least I could sit at the table with the adults and soak in the memories. Coffee always has been a part of my life, but it was only by accident that I discovered what a big role coffee played in St. Louis's history.

While researching another book, *A Culinary History of Missouri: Foodways & Iconic Dishes of the Show-Me State* (The History Press), I stumbled on a 2015 interview from our local National Public Radio station about an exhibit at the Missouri History Museum in St. Louis. The exhibit, "Coffee: The World in Your Cup and St. Louis in Your Cup," highlighted the fact that in the early 1900s, St. Louis was the coffee capital of the country; the city was the largest inland distributor of coffee in the United States and one of the busiest in the world. I knew we had coffee companies here, but I'd never heard that prestigious designation in all the years I've lived in St. Louis. And I wasn't alone in this. When I share this historical tidbit with people in my circle of friends, I always hear, "I didn't know that!"

I was fortunate to sit down in March with the exhibit's curator, Katie Moon, who said the rich coffee history in St. Louis also took her by surprise as she worked on the exhibit. "The fact that it [coffee history] existed at all; I mean I knew about Kaldi's [a current St. Louis coffee company], but it [coffee] was such an economic boon and had a far-reaching appeal," she said.

St. Louis's fascinating coffee history was fueled by risk-takers, creatives and hardworking families. But as part of the global coffee movement in the eighteenth and nineteenth centuries, the horrific history of colonial plantations with their enslaved workforces came with every bag of green coffee that was brought upriver.

Today's coffee culture is vibrant with plentiful opportunities to find and sip that perfect cup. So, pour yourself a mug and let's explore this story together.

ACKNOWLEDGEMENTS

A huge amount of gratitude goes to several people at the Missouri Historical Society (MHS). Katie Moon, exhibits manager, was generous with her time as well as sharing research with me. Other MHS staff to whom I am grateful include Dennis Northcott, associate archivist; Lauren Mitchell, director of publications; Madeline Reichmuth, public information officer; Amanda Clark, community tours manager; and Lauren Sallwasser, associate photo archivist.

Thanks also to Sara Hodge, curator of the Herman T. Pott National Inland Waterways Collection at the St. Louis Mercantile Library.

I raise my coffee cup to all the St. Louis coffee roasters who were so generous in giving their time for interviews, posing for photos and, most important, creating a vibrant coffee culture for our area. They all are integral components to the neighborhoods in which they make their home, and St. Louis is so much richer for their work.

Finally, my thanks to Chad Rhoad, acquisitions editor, and to the team at The History Press for their expertise and support as they journeyed with me toward completion of this project. I'm pleased that St. Louis now can join other notable coffee cities like New Orleans, New York and San Francisco in the American Palate series.

INTRODUCTION

I t's a Wednesday afternoon in late November, and Maplewood Deli and Coffeehouse is humming with activity. Couples and friends sit across from one another engaged in what look to be fascinating conversations. A few people have laptops and sit alone, sipping a cup of coffee as they work. This welcoming place, formerly known as Foundation Grounds, is one of dozens of coffeehouses in St. Louis that helped brew the city's third coffee wave.

But it's a safe bet that most customers enjoying an espresso, latte or macchiato at their favorite coffeehouse aren't aware of St. Louis's rich coffee history. Let's be honest: We tend to take the food and drink consumed daily for granted because it's simply a part of our routines. According to 2022 statistics from the National Coffee Association—which has its roots in St. Louis—66 percent of Americans drink coffee every day, up 14 percent since January 2021. Coffee consumption in the United States is at a two-decade high according to the association's statistics.

Since its beginnings as a French fur-trading post, coffee has been a part of St. Louis business and family life. At first, coffee was a luxury brought from New Orleans to Pierre Laclède and Auguste Chouteau's fur-trade outpost, but the coffee industry exploded in St. Louis following the Civil War, resulting in many innovations that helped bring coffee to our tables. Eventually, St. Louis was the largest inland distributor of coffee in the United States.

And while it largely was a man's game, the city's first female executives worked for a coffee company. Our more recent history includes the hip coffeehouses of Gaslight Square. And who can forget those iconic Dana Brown or Old Judge commercials?

We'll also look at notable coffee roasters and companies operating today. While Ronnoco has been in business here for over one hundred years, others have made their mark on the city in just a few years' time. By the end of the book, I hope you will have interesting tales to share at your next coffee klatsch, whether it's around your kitchen table or with your neighborhood barista.

THE FRENCH CONNECTION

Besides the beauty of the site, he [Pierre Laclède] *found there
all the advantages that one could desire to found a settlement
which might become very considerable hereafter.*
—*August Chouteau*

Pierre Laclède was about as far away from home as a man could be. The Frenchman arrived in New Orleans in 1755 and was a partner in the New Orleans firm Maxent, Laclède and Company. Tasked with setting up a trading post in Upper Louisiana, Laclède saw a spot of land on the western bank of the Mississippi River in November 1763 and knew it would be ideal. This spot, about twelve miles south of the Missouri River confluence, would be perfect, and he wasted no time claiming it.

Laclède and his men spent the winter on the east side of the Mississippi River near Fort Chartres, but by February 1764, he had sent his fourteen-year-old stepson, Auguste Chouteau, and a band of about thirty men to return to "where we notched the trees" to clear land and build a storage shed for provisions and cabins to house the workmen. By April, Laclède had returned to select the location of his home and headquarters. He also carried plans for laying out the village that he named after King Louis IX of France.

The fur-trading community was closely designed after other French colonial cities of the time, most likely New Orleans. Laclède marked the

Left: Pierre Lacléde portrait. *Right*: Auguste Chouteau portrait from the late eighteenth century. *Missouri Historical Society, St. Louis.*

settlement in rectangular blocks, stretching about a half mile north to south and three blocks west from the Mississippi River. As noted by William Barnaby Faherty, a Jesuit historian and author, the block closest to the river was the parade ground. The next block west was used for Laclède's headquarters, and the third block was set aside for a church. Common fields and some land for settlers also were part of the settlement. There was no retail center, but St. Louis had two granaries, a bakery and a maple sugar works. Keelboats from New Orleans brought necessary cargo, including flour, sugar, whiskey, household goods and probably coffee.

Another Frenchman, Clement Delor de Treget, along with resident farmers from Illinois, settled south of St. Louis in 1771, creating "Delor's Village," later renamed Carondelet in honor of Francisco Héctor de Carondelet, then governor general of Louisiana. The land grant Delor received included a narrow strip of land for the "common fields." Most Carondelet residents were farmers or woodcutters; its population in 1799 of 184 people was reported to Spanish officials. St. Louis, by comparison, tallied 925 residents for the 1799 census. Although a rivalry between the two villages had developed, they exchanged goods and services—perhaps most important for St. Louis, flour from Carondelet.

But St. Louis trade was successful. As historian Fred Fausz, associate professor emeritus at the University of Missouri–St. Louis, told *Missouri Conservationist*, St. Louis was "a noisy, smelly, violent and raucous place." Laclède and Chouteau developed agreements with the Indigenous people of the area, especially the Osage, who provided fur and hides to Laclède and company in exchange for items such as muskets, knives, kettles and European foods brought up the river from New Orleans. From 1772 to 1775, traders sent more than six hundred thousand pounds of hides and furs downriver.

After Laclède's death in 1778, Chouteau took over and grew the business. The family's affluence was readily visible by their large estate with the two-story home and headquarters at the center. By 1789, Chouteau had rebuilt Laclède's home into the largest house in St. Louis. Chouteau's home featured furniture from Europe, walnut flooring, silver tableware and a crystal chandelier. It is described as a two-story stone structure in a square bordered by Market Street to the north, Main Street to the east, Walnut Street to the south and Second Street to the west. According to historian and author James F. McDermott, Chouteau's home also included a massive personal library that contained more than six hundred volumes at the time of his death in 1829. The Chouteaus' lifestyle in St. Louis was so grand that William Henry Harrison, then governor of the Indiana Territory, wrote to a friend after visiting in 1804 that it "rivaled those of first rank in Philadelphia or New York."

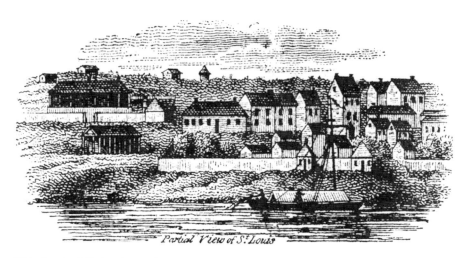

This sketch of St. Louis as a fur-trading post was made in 1814, appearing on the back of a banknote in 1817. *Wikimedia Commons*.

John Caspar Wild created a lithograph in 1841 of the Chouteau mansion in St. Louis. *Wikimedia Commons*.

As the richest family in town and one that entertained visiting dignitaries, the Chouteaus would have had no trouble procuring the luxuries of the day from France via New Orleans, such as French wines and coffee. It's not hard to imagine the Chouteau men enjoying coffee and brandy in the library after dinner.

In contrast, most of St. Louis's homes were built of vertical logs, *poteaux-en-terre* (posts in ground). These were the residences of the city's tradesmen, boatmen and workmen. The lots for homes such as these were a half acre, enough space for outbuildings such as kitchens and barns. Small gardens with space for fruit trees were included in these homesites, which were enclosed by six-foot-high wooden fences.

But whether a family was rich or poor, French families in St. Louis—and in other French settlements in Missouri, such as Ste. Genevieve—set the finest table they could afford. A meal for Missouri's French Creoles was more than simply sustenance; it was one of life's pleasures. This appreciation for food and its preparation was noted by Henry Brackenridge in his 1834 account *Reflections of the West*: "[T]he humblest of French cooks possessed an appreciation of the culinary arts and a mastery of cookery."

Creole cooks learned to create meals from what was available, and catfish was a favorite ingredient for a main meal. African-inspired gumbos plus

This silver coffee pot from 1815 was owned by the Chouteau family. *Missouri Historical Society, St. Louis.*

stews, soups, fricassees and bread made from locally grown and milled wheat would have been common foods.

French Canadians helped establish apple orchards, which made desserts such as fruit tarts possible. And meals were often accompanied by local beers and ciders, wine from France or Spain and coffee if it was available. If a family was fortunate to get green coffee beans from New Orleans, the woman of the house first had to roast them in a skillet over a fire for about twenty minutes. If that was successful, the browned and cracked beans were ground by hand using a mortar and pestle and strained before brewing in three to four ounces of boiling water. The result: a mug of coffee as brown and thick as the Mississippi River.

For wealthy families such as the Chouteaus, enslaved house servants brewed the coffee and transferred it from a metal kettle to an ornate serving set. The coffee then would have been poured for the family and guests into delicate porcelain cups held by matching saucers.

Whether sipped from a china cup in a parlor or from a tin cup on a fur-trading expedition, coffee was among the variety of goods brought upriver to St. Louis from New Orleans. However, the source of these beans shines a light on the dark side of coffee.

Top Off Your Cup: The Museum at the Gateway Arch

To get a feel for colonial life in eighteenth-century St. Louis, visit the Museum at the Gateway Arch. More than two hundred years of history is explored in six themed areas at the museum, which opened in 2018 as part of a $380 million renovation to the national park. In the area about the earliest days in St. Louis, visitors can see a replicated small French Creole home and a wooden canoe like those used to navigate the Mississippi River at the time. Despite its size, the home likely would have been built by hired craftsmen. For more information, visit www.archpark.org.

Top: An example of a canoe that would have been used during colonial times in St. Louis for navigating the Mississippi River can be seen at the Museum at the Gateway Arch. *Gateway Arch*.

Bottom: The Museum at the Gateway Arch. *Gateway Arch*.

COFFEE'S BITTER TALE

Although it's not known exactly when or by whom coffee was discovered, most historians believe Ethiopia (ancient Abyssinia) to be the birthplace. Several legends attempt to explain this discovery, with the story of Ethiopian goatherd Kaldi being the most accepted. When Kaldi's goats didn't respond to his calling them home, he found them nibbling on an unusual shrub with dark green leaves and red berries. The animals exhibited renewed playful energy from the nontoxic shrub, so Kaldi tried the berries and started dancing with his goats.

Trade routes pushed coffee out into the world, first to Arabia and then to Europe. The tragic aspect of coffee's history is tied to global colonialism and the enslavement of Indigenous and African people. Later, revolutions in France and in some of its coffee-producing colonies impacted St. Louis's French culture.

By the mid-1500s, coffee was being exported throughout the Turkish empire and coffeehouses were in Constantinople (today's Istanbul), serving residents, merchants and world travelers. Whether coffee was deemed the devil's drink or that of the gods, the desire for the drink grew strong.

In *New Orleans Coffee*, author Suzanne Stone writes that coffee was in most of Europe in the 1600s. Merchant Pierre de la Roque is credited with introducing coffee to France in 1644, as he brought coffee beans from Turkey to Marseille. In 1671, the first French coffeehouse opened, and within fifty years, coffee was a beloved beverage. Even Voltaire called coffee his muse. By the time St. Louis was founded, Paris had three thousand cafés that sold coffee, according to the Missouri Historical Society.

By the mid-seventeenth century, London had three hundred coffeehouses—"penny universities," as they were sometimes called—according to the National Coffee Association. But by 1675, that number reached nearly three thousand. The first coffeehouse in America opened in Boston in 1676, and about one hundred years later, coffee was regularly sold in New Orleans by *vendeuses* (street vendors), who often were enslaved women working to buy their freedom. It's likely the beans those women were roasting to make their coffee came from the West Indies, including Saint-Domingue, which was a French colony from 1659 to 1804 on the Caribbean Island of Hispaniola. That island today is home to the Dominican Republic and Haiti.

Gabriel Mathieu de Clieu, a naval officer serving on Martinique, in 1720 or 1723 obtained seedlings from a coffee plant in Jardin des Plantes in Paris given to the French government by the Dutch in 1714 and successfully planted them on the island. Although coffee cultivation had been introduced to Saint-Domingue in 1715, these hardier plants from Martinique flourished. By 1788, Saint-Domingue, also known as San Domingo, was supplying coffee to half the world, according to author Mark Pendergrast.

An engraving depicting Gabriel de Clieu tending a coffee plant. *Wikimedia Commons*.

Coffee plantations in European colonies in the Caribbean, Asia and Central and South America were powered by enslaved workers, whether Indigenous or from Africa. These workers lived in horrific conditions and were beaten and sometimes killed by white oppressors. Everyday life for coffee plantation enslaved laborers meant living in windowless huts, not getting enough food and being worked literally to death. Conditions for enslaved workers on coffee plantations in Spanish colonies including Brazil were similarly horrible. According to Princeton University, Brazil enslaved Indigenous people and Africans until the 1860s. Of the 12 million Africans brought to the New World, 5.5 million were enslaved in Brazil between 1540 and the mid-nineteenth century.

The middle and upper classes in Europe and America sipped coffee and discussed politics in their cafés, but at what human cost?

Saint-Domingue enslaved persons rose up in 1791 during a countrywide revolution that lasted nearly thirteen years. This had an impact on eighteenth-century Missouri. During the uprising, some French made their way to the Louisiana Territory. It's estimated that as many as ten thousand French left their sugar and coffee plantations on the island to come to America. Some families settled on the East Coast in New Jersey and Pennsylvania; it's not known how many decided to come west, but a few families settled in St. Louis.

One of the first to arrive in St. Louis may have been Francois Barousel. According to Dorothy Garesché Holland, whose French ancestors came from Saint-Domingue, Barousel arrived in St. Louis from Saint-Domingue in 1796 but soon relocated to Ste. Genevieve, Missouri. On his death in 1797, Barousel left his U.S. assets to his Philadelphia business partner, Nicholas Lesconfleure, while his personal possessions in France were given to his brothers and sisters. One of his nieces, Adelaide Barousel, left Baltimore to live with a friend in St. Louis. She married Michel Desravines Tesson to establish one of St. Louis's successful nineteenth-century families.

Like his bride, Tesson was born in Saint-Dominique. Orphaned during the revolt, the young child was rescued by an enslaved man and was hidden in his cabin, according to Holland. Tesson (and possibly his two older brothers) was put on a ship for America in 1793.

Tesson lived with a French family in Philadelphia for a few years and there studied English. Learning about opportunities in St. Louis, the young man relocated to the city in 1810. He and Adelaide Barousel were married in 1811 and had two children, Edward and Coralie. Tesson became a successful merchant and was awarded a military title by Governor William

This photo by Marc Ferrez shows slaves on a coffee farm in Brazil in 1885. *Wikimedia Commons.*

A map from 1810 of the French colony Saint-Domingue. *Wikimedia Commons.*

Clark in 1817. However, Tesson's health prompted him to move his family to a milder climate, New Orleans, where he died in 1845.

Jules Louis René de Mun was born on April 25, 1782, in Saint-Domingue. His parents, the Vicomte Bernard Jacques and Madeleine de Mun, left France for the island just ahead of the French Revolution. The family returned so Jules and his brother Auguste could go to school in France. But the revolution strengthened, and the parents fled to England. A nurse helped the boys get out of France and rejoin their parents.

De Mun, his widowed mother and his brother relocated to Cuba around 1803, and while the family had petitioned the country for citizenship, de Mun sailed for America in 1809, living first in New Jersey before coming to St. Louis about a year later. He married Louise Isabelle Apoline Gratiot, daughter of Charles and Victoire Chouteau Gratiot, in 1812. The couple lived for a time in Ste. Genevieve, where he operated a successful store. De Mun joined Auguste Pierre Chouteau on a trading expedition in 1816 and later went into business with Chouteau but left the company after a year. He worked briefly in retail before leaving St. Louis with his family to return to Cuba, where he grew coffee. The family came back to the United States in 1831. He was the recorder of deeds for the County of St. Louis when he died in 1843.

Another son of Saint-Domingue had an impact on St. Louis. Louis William DuBourg was born in 1766 to Pierre and Marguerite DuBourg. His father was a successful merchant, possibly in the coffee trade, and a sea captain. After the death of his mother, DuBourg lived with his maternal grandparents in Bourdeaux, France, and received his education in Paris from the Sulpicians, a clerical order.

DuBourg's passion as a priest was education, and after he came to St. Louis from New Orleans in 1817, he was instrumental in the establishment of Saint Louis University, Academy of the Sacred Heart in St. Charles, Missouri, and St. Mary's of the Barrens near Perryville, Missouri.

Clearly, the coffee beans coming into St. Louis in the eighteenth and nineteenth centuries were sourced from colonial plantations that utilized enslaved workers and unethical labor practices. But what about today? How have labor practices surrounding coffee changed?

The Sustainable Coffee Challenge is a movement launched in 2015 by Conservation International and 18 founding partners, including Starbucks. Today, 155 partners are a part of this global movement. Evidence of forced labor, human trafficking and child labor still exist within our coffee supply.

While the world's top-producing coffee countries—Brazil, Vietnam, Colombia, Indonesia and Ethiopia—have national action plans to fight forced and child labor, these policies are only as good as their enforcement. For more information, visit www.sustaincoffee.org.

Top Off Your Cup: Make Informed Coffee Purchases

According to the National Coffee Association, Americans drink an estimated 517 million cups of coffee per day. But what do you know about your favorite coffee brand and how the beans are sourced? Tools are available to consumers to help them make responsible purchases. Look up national brands online. If you purchase coffee from a St. Louis business, ask where the beans are coming from. Many roasters today are in partnership with the small family farms that produce coffee, so just ask a few questions about how the beans are sourced.

In St. Louis, Washington University's Green Office Program in 2020 published an article that described some of the labels to look for when purchasing coffee. The Fair Trade Certified label indicates that the coffee has met high social, economic and environmental standards. The Rainforest Alliance label indicates that the coffee's source is engaged in biodiversity conservation, community development and the fair treatment of its farmers. Plus, all Rainforest Alliance farms are "shade-grown," which has the lowest impact on the environment.

Through a little research, you can make confident purchases and fully enjoy that cup of coffee.

3

AN INDUSTRY IS BORN

There's always something happening on the St. Louis riverfront. The one-and-a-half-mile promenade and bike path are popular with downtown visitors and residents for exercise any time of the year. The iconic Gateway Arch and its outstanding museum attract visitors and residents year-round. Nearby Laclede's Landing, always evolving, offers dining and entertainment options. Catch a scenic riverboat cruise during spring through fall months.

St. Louis's riverfront has changed since Pierre Laclède's arrival, but the growth the city experienced in the 1800s, thanks in large part to steamboats and railroads, was as monumental as the modern Gateway Arch's presence.

By the early nineteenth century, St. Louis was sitting in the catbird seat. The fur trade remained strong, and the Chouteaus were considered the "royal family of the wilderness." When the Louisiana Purchase was completed in 1803, the city's population was less than one thousand people. Richard Edwards in *Great West* details the Chouteaus. Auguste and his stepbrother, Pierre, were the principal traders. Pierre Chouteau's compound, which included a fruit orchard, was encircled with a stone wall, "and the house and store were in one building, the store being the first store and the family residence the second."

Given the cost of importing goods and the price to transport the cargo upriver, the price for items like sugar and coffee in 1803 was two dollars per pound, so it remained a luxury for many. Once steamboats opened the riverways to trade, coffee prices fell to around fifty cents per pound by 1816.

St. Louis was incorporated in 1809 with a population of 1,400, and the town grew rapidly. With the start of the next decade, St. Louis saw more immigrants from European countries like Ireland and Germany. New business, including banking and printing, sprang up in the city. Irish immigrant Joseph Charless introduced the first newspaper west of the Mississippi, the *Missouri Gazette*, in 1808. St. Louis saw its first steamboat, the *Zebulon Pike*, arrive on August 2, 1817.

By 1822, five thousand people made St. Louis their home within its 385 acres. The city had three weekly newspapers, three large inns and several small taverns and a handful of other businesses. But most significant, fifty-seven grocers were doing business in St. Louis, and the grocery trade would become the city's economic backbone. The city incorporated in 1823.

Hundreds of steamboats made daily stops in St. Louis by the 1850s, bringing with them a variety of goods, including coffee. In its Annual Statement of Trade and Commerce, the Merchants' Exchange of St. Louis reported that 78,842 sacks of coffee had been imported in 1848, a "fair portion" of which was intended for Chicago and "other towns on the lake." A bill of lading from January 1849 showed 152 bags of coffee were shipped from New Orleans to R.A. (Robert) Barnes on the steamboat *Highlander*. Barnes, a wholesale grocer at the time, would go on to become a local bank president in St. Louis. His bequest when he died in 1892 helped to build Barnes Hospital, now Barnes-Jewish Hospital, an affiliate teaching hospital of Washington University.

Railroads brought goods to St. Louis from both coasts. Accessible transportation and a central location made Missouri, which had become a state in 1821, a popular stop for miners, trappers and settlers heading west. As early as the 1830s, wholesalers set up warehouses to service companies that in turn were doing a healthy outfitting business. By the 1840s, offices and warehouses of wholesale grocers lined the riverfront. Hundreds of steamboats made daily stops in St. Louis by the 1850s. According to *The Illustrated Miners' Hand-book and Guide to Pike's Peak* (1859): "Saint Louis is the Great Central Outfitting Point, for Miners and western Emigrants.…This city, as the Metropolis of the Mississippi Valley, has no rival in the West, in point of trade and commerce."

Coffee, once a luxury, was now a common household item, as well as something to be included in one's outfit for the trek west. Companies like Menown's Tea, Coffee and Spice Emporium advertised a variety of items with which to stock one's wagon, including roasted coffee that could also be ground and packaged in any size desired. People preparing to head

This model of St. Louis's riverfront during its steamboat era can be seen at the Museum at the Gateway Arch. *Gateway Arch.*

west could get almost anything in St. Louis, from wagons to tin pans to flour. Coffee stands were also found in 1871 at public markets, including City, Centre and Soulard. The latter is still open and doing business in the city.

But coffee wasn't found just at general stores, public markets and on the wagons of traders and prospectors. Coffeehouses were thriving; more than fifty were listed in the 1845 city directory. Two of the oldest, Leonhard's and Speck's, were located on Market Street. Conrad Leonhard and Jacob Speck opened their establishments in 1844. Both were famous for their coffee and coffee cake. Men came each afternoon to have their coffee and cigar upstairs while women gathered for "coffee parties." Around the turn of the century, H.G. Goerner bought both restaurants, relocating Leonhard's to North Eighth Street.

The city battled a cholera epidemic in 1849 as well as a devastating fire that tore through the riverfront area along Third Street, causing more than $6 million in damage. A steamboat broke loose and spread the fire to more than twenty additional boats. Freight on the levee also fueled the fire.

But coffee was here to stay, and visionary businessmen would emerge to begin an industry.

Pioneers in St. Louis Coffee

In 1853, St. Louis had a population of more than seventy-seven thousand and was expanding to the south and west. Washington University was a newly incorporated educational institution. The Pacific Railroad yards were being built at the old site of Chouteau's Pond, which had been drained following the cholera outbreak.

This also was the year when David Nicholson, a successful grocer, opened Franklin Tea and Coffee House near North Fourth Street and Broadway. Nicholson's plan was to roast coffee with steam power and sell it to consumers to use in their homes. The steam engine and coffee mills were displayed in the window.

Although some home kitchens would have new coffee roasters brought to the area by German immigrants, green coffee beans primarily were purchased in bulk at general stores and roasted in homes either in an oven or on top of the stove in shallow pans. The idea to commercially roast the beans by a machine was new and likely a bit strange to Nicholson's customers, which may have in part led to the failure of his coffee roasting business less than a year after opening.

Nicholson's tea, coffee and sugar warehouse business continued, but he sold the coffee roasting business to fellow grocer James H. Forbes in 1853.

An example of an early coffee roasting machine from 1884. *Missouri Historical Society, St. Louis.*

An immigrant from Scotland, Forbes knew that selling the idea of roasted coffee to St. Louis consumers would be an uphill battle, but he believed it was an idea whose time had come. He approached the marketing campaign with the idea that pre-roasted coffee saves money, fuel and labor. Given that consumers were buying bulk coffee for about twelve cents per pound (comparatively, sugar was four cents per pound) in 1853 and using at-home roasting methods that often resulted in burnt beans and bitter coffee, a pre-roasted bag of coffee for twenty-five cents might save a housewife time, trouble and embarrassment. Forbes also roasted coffee for wholesalers at a penny a pound.

In 1857, Forbes's son Alexander began working in the store after school and was made a partner in 1870. Another son, Robert, joined the business—known as James Forbes, Coffee Merchant—in 1878. Founder James Forbes died in 1891. Soon after, his sons, now running the company, decided to discontinue the retail coffee business, renamed the firm James H. Forbes Tea and Coffee Company and sold coffee and tea on a wholesale basis. By 1893, the company needed more space and moved from its original location to 112 Locust Street. In 1898, a spice department was added.

In the mid-1800s, another immigrant found his way to St. Louis. David G. Evans, born in South Wales, was employed by the W. & J.G. Flint Company, coffee roasters based in Milwaukee, Wisconsin. The firm opened a plant in St. Louis, Flint-Crocker Company, with Evans as an employee, in 1858. He rose through the ranks and became a partner in what became the Flint-Evans Company. The firm's name later was changed to the David G. Evans Company. Like other roasters of the day, the company packaged and sold teas and spices, but the Old Judge coffee brand was the building block of Evans's business.

An article in the *St. Louis Globe-Democrat* marking the one hundredth anniversary of Old Judge noted that Evans blended coffee beans that arrived at the St. Louis riverfront and stored them in the Old Judge warehouse. Company salesmen every morning showed up at the warehouse to load their horse-drawn wagons with coffee beans. The salesmen visited grocers and "large commercial users of coffee" in the morning to deliver roasted beans and returned in the afternoon to pick up orders for the following day.

William Schotten was another coffee pioneer. Born in 1820 in Duesseldorf, Germany, Schotten had built a reputation for making outstanding mustard, a culinary staple in Germany since medieval times. Joining the early wave of German immigrants in the mid-1830s and 1840s, Schotten relocated his life and mustard business to St. Louis.

At first, Schotten sold his hand-ground mustard from a basket at his stand in Center Market House, which stood at Spruce and Poplar Streets. He soon could afford to purchase a horse and wagon and sold his product across the city. By 1847, he was able to open a small factory on South Third Street. He also operated a gristmill on North Market Street, although that would later be destroyed by fire.

Schotten married Wilhelmina "Mina" Herberg in 1857. The couple had four children, Hubertus, Julius, Henry and Henriette. By 1860, Schotten's brother Christian had joined him as partner, and the company was known as William Schotten and Company.

The company started roasting coffee in 1862. After Christian died, Schotten took on Henry Vesborg as partner in 1867. By the time of its fiftieth anniversary in 1897, the company had moved into a new building on Broadway and Clark, where it roasted its three coffee blends (Sinbad, Golden Days and Queen's Table) and manufactured baking powder, culinary herbs, ketchup, sauces and tea.

When William died in 1875, sons Hubertus and Julius entered the family business. Hubertus died in 1898, leaving Julius Schotten—a graduate of St. Louis University who was described as an intelligent businessman with great integrity—as the sole proprietor. He later became the company's first president and earned a national reputation in the coffee industry.

Julius shared with author William Ukers tales about the "early days" of the business, when wholesale grocers controlled 90 percent of the coffee trade and most of Schotten's business was roasting coffee for them at a penny a pound. Most grocers bought the coffee in five- and ten-pound packages, which lasted in their store for about a week. He told Ukers that most of the green coffee in St. Louis came from Brazil and Jamaica.

A portrait of Julius Schotten, 1910. He was president of William Schotten Coffee Company. *Missouri Historical Society, St. Louis.*

Other German immigrants had success in St. Louis's early coffee industry. The Steinwender-Stoffregen Coffee Company dates to January 2, 1876, when Julius Steinwender and brothers Herman and Charles Stoffregen formed a partnership to purchase a coffee roasting and spice business from Louis Ritsert. The new firm moved from Morgan Street to a larger location on North Fourth Street.

Born in 1843, Steinwender and his parents left Berlin, Germany, when he was eight years old. Raised and educated in St. Louis, it's not clear how he met the Stoffregen brothers, but their coffee business grew large enough that Steinwender moved to New York in 1885 to manage their eastern branch, housed on Wall Street. By 1902, the New York branch ranked fifth among coffee importers. Eventually, the company had branches all over the world, including in London and Brazil, as well as in Chicago, Cincinnati, New Orleans, Milwaukee and Philadelphia. Yale was the flagship brand of Steinwender-Stoffregen.

Charles Stoffregen was born on July 9, 1851, in Lippstadt, Germany, and came to St. Louis when he was fourteen years old. He attended night school to learn English and worked in a brewery for twenty-five dollars a month. He later opened a grocery business with his brother in 1873. In an interview with the *St. Louis Post-Dispatch*, Stoffregen said he always saved money, even while working as a clerk at the brewery. Herman Stoffregen left the coffee and grocery trade to become an executive with Koken Realty Company.

Irish immigrant William J. Kinsella carved a place in St. Louis history. Born in Carlow, Ireland, in 1846 to Patrick and Ellen Kinsella, he attended St. Patrick's College in Carlow and started his long career with a Dublin wholesaler. At the age of nineteen, Kinsella crossed the Atlantic Ocean to seek his fortune in New York and Baltimore before settling down in Cleveland, Ohio, in 1870 to start a grocery business with his brother Edward.

William moved to St. Louis in 1874 and worked for two companies before being hired in 1879 by the Thompson-Taylor Spice Company of Chicago to start its St. Louis operation. He purchased the business just two years later and reorganized the firm under the banner William J. Kinsella & Company. The business incorporated in 1886 with a capital stock of $250,000 and became Hanley & Kinsella Coffee & Spice Company. Over time, the firm had two factories on Spruce Street; annual sales reached $1.5 million.

Kinsella also was involved in banking. He was director of the Mechanics National Bank as well as the Mercantile Trust Company. In 1895, he became a member of the St. Louis Merchants Exchange. A civic-minded man, Kinsella was active with several agencies, leagues and clubs.

Kinsella married Nellie Hanley of New York City in 1880. The couple had three children, William J. Jr., Dalton and Ella. Kinsella groomed his eldest, William, to be his successor. After graduating from the University of Notre Dame in 1900, William Jr. began his career with his father's company.

Another coffee pioneer, Cyrus F. Blanke, was born on October 24, 1862, in Marine, Illinois. After attending commercial college in St. Louis, Blanke was ready to begin a business career. At sixteen, he worked as a grocery clerk but moved to a wholesale tobacco factory. Before his twentieth birthday, Blanke was working in collections for Steinwender-Stoffregen Coffee Company, steeping himself in the tea, coffee and spice business. Two years later, he moved into sales and traveled for seven years. He married Eugenia Frowein in 1889, and in 1890, Blanke left his sales position to start his own firm, C.F. Blanke Tea and Coffee Company. After eight years, Blanke's company grew to be one of the biggest coffee roasting businesses in the "west," and its product reached across the country. His premium brand, Faust coffee, was offered at Tony Faust's celebrated St. Louis restaurant, and by 1899, the brand was part of the dining service on the Wabash Railroad. He'd eventually spin off other companies, including St. Louis Tin and Sheet Metal, enabling Blanke to produce his own coffee cans.

A fire in September 1895 at the company's South Second Street site resulted in $45,000 in losses, although firemen saved the horses, delivery wagons and buggies. The fire started in an exhaust pipe on one of the coffee roasters. The coffee, tea and spice stock was a total loss, but Blanke's company relocated to a new building on Seventh Street and went on to have huge impacts at the St. Louis World's Fair and beyond.

Frederick Roth Sr. came to the United States from Germany as a young child in 1856 and attended St. Louis public schools. His first job as a grocery clerk led him to a career in coffee sales in 1885. Herman August Homeyer was born in Germany in 1860. He started at age fifteen in the grocery business and worked eight years. He came to the United States in 1884 and worked in the wholesale grocery and toy businesses before moving to Steinwender-Stoffregen, where he eventually became secretary of the corporation.

Roth, Homeyer and associates organized Roth-Homeyer Coffee Company in 1898. The wholesalers had offices on North Second Street, where they roasted coffee and traded teas and spices. They developed the Steer brand and Holland coffee blend.

Nash-Smith Tea and Coffee Company, established in 1868 by Michael E. Smith and Charles Espenschied, was located on North Sixth Street. Smith, who was born in Ireland, came to St. Louis in 1865 and began business as a grocery clerk for Nash Brothers. Smith and Espenchied purchased Eagle Spice Mills from the executors of Mathew Hunt, who operated that business until his death in 1868. According to a 1925 edition of the *Tea and Coffee Trade Journal*, George Nash, who had previously retired from the grocery business to join his brother in Texas, returned to St. Louis to join the coffee firm Nash-

Smith and Espenschied. When Espenschied retired in 1878, the company's name became Nash-Smith and Company, which was updated in 1888 and incorporated as Nash-Smith Tea and Coffee Company. Its principal brand was Wedding Breakfast coffee, which was distributed throughout the West, Southwest and Northwest.

A funny story involving one of the company's salesmen, Matthew King, was reported in the October 29, 1895 edition of the *St. Louis Post-Dispatch*. According to the newspaper, King parked his horse and buggy in front of a grocer on North Second Street and went inside to sell the owner coffee and tea. While conducting his business, King heard the wheels of his buggy rattle as it moved away from the curb. When he ran outside, he saw two unidentified young women driving off with his horse and buggy.

He ran after them, shouting, "Stop 'em! Stop the horse thieves," but the women got away, with one of them shouting, "We'll get even with them yet!"

After reporting the theft to the police and to his employer, King told the newspaper he was offended by the young women's action, that they should have "appropriated the horse and buggy and samples without getting introduced in the proper style." Later, the horse and buggy were found tied to a tree with a note pinned to the seat: "We are sorry for this, but everything is all O.K. Do not let it go any further." It's not known what happened to King's coffee and tea samples.

Brothers Robert and Alfred Meyer of Franklin County, Missouri, launched Meyer Brothers Coffee Company in 1899. Alfred sold his shares to Robert in 1918 but returned to the coffee business in 1922 with his own firm, A.H. Meyer Coffee Company. However, that business was sold in 1928, and at the time of his death in 1937, Alfred worked for Reliance Life Insurance. Meyer Brothers Coffee, a wholesaler, also distributed Old Judge, the flagship brand for David G. Evans Coffee Company, which bought out Meyer Brothers in 1929.

MAKING COFFEE AT HOME

Think about your morning coffee routine for a moment. If you're like most Americans, you scoop the desired amount of ground coffee from a bag or canister on your counter, pour the required amount of water into your automatic coffee maker and press the brew button. In a few minutes, a hot and delicious mug of coffee is at your disposal. This certainly wasn't the case two hundred years ago.

Unroasted coffee was sold in bulk by grocers. Often, foreign objects, including sawdust, stones and even trash, were hidden among the beans. Coffee was roasted in a heavy pan on top of a stove or in an oven, often resulting in varying results; as noted by Eliza Leslie in *Directions for Cookery* (1840 edition), pan roasting caused the beans' flavor to evaporate. Another option for mid-nineteenth-century coffee drinkers was to purchase roasted coffee from their grocer. When the coffee was ready to grind, the beans might be smashed with a rolling pin or an iron skillet and then boiled in a tin coffee pot for as long as thirty minutes.

Directions for Cookery goes on to explain that it's best for households to own a coffee roaster and mill. It was recommended that coffee be added a spoonful at a time to the coffee pot, stirring frequently. An egg white would sometimes be added. When it had risen to the top, the pot was removed a bit off the fire but allowed to continue boiling. Eventually, a "teacup of cold water" would be added before the coffee rested for ten minutes. Silver or china coffee pots intended for service would be scalded before the coffee was slowly poured to avoid disturbing the grounds.

This photo from 1880 by St. Louis photographer Emil Boehl captures his wife and other women enjoying coffee in a backyard. *Missouri Historical Society, St. Louis.*

By the mid-nineteenth century, coffee roasters were becoming important kitchen tools. Roasters were usually made of cast iron with a handle connected to a blade inside the roaster that moved the beans around to prevent burning. The roaster was set on top of a stove. Up to a pound of green coffee could be roasted at a time. Coffee mills were commonly seen in homes by the 1880s. The beans would be poured into the top of the mill, and a hand crank forced them through the grinding mechanism, depositing the grounds in a bottom drawer. Wall-mounted glass coffee grinders, considered to be more modern, appeared around the 1900s.

Retailers such as Simmons Hardware provided St. Louis households with coffee-related products, such as roasters, mills and pots. The store published an annual leather-bound catalog with gold leaf detail that included pages and pages of items such as these. Simmons Hardware Company opened for business in 1874. From 1879 to 1895, it occupied a five-story brick building at Ninth Street and Washington Avenue. A business listing in the 1900 edition of *Gould's Commercial Register* places Simmons Hardware's retail location at 212 North Broadway and its wholesale/warehouse at 900 Spruce Street.

Local manufacturing companies also jumped on coffee's bandwagon. Brothers Frederick and William Niedringhaus were part of the wave of German immigrants who arrived in St. Louis in the 1850s. The brothers, both tinsmiths by trade, emigrated in 1855. Just four years later, they began a tinworks to manufacture household goods. Business grew, and by 1865, they had incorporated as the St. Louis Stamping Company and built a factory on Second Street and Cass Avenue.

But the product that brought them great success and national fame was graniteware, also known as granite ironware. While visiting Europe, William found similar pots and pans and studied for weeks at the European factory to learn about the process. Armed with the knowledge, he returned to St. Louis in 1874 and began graniteware production; U.S. patents for the process and products were received in 1876 and 1877.

Demand for the durable cookware became so great that the brothers could build their own ironworks, Granite Iron Rolling Mills, in St. Louis in 1878. By the late 1880s, they had a successful way to enamel tin as well as iron. The graniteware coffee pots were both practical and attractive, allowing coffee to be brewed and served in the same vessel.

With business booming, St. Louis Stamping Company and its mill needed to expand in the 1890s. Thanks to cheaper land on the east side of the Mississippi River—as well as access to transportation and more

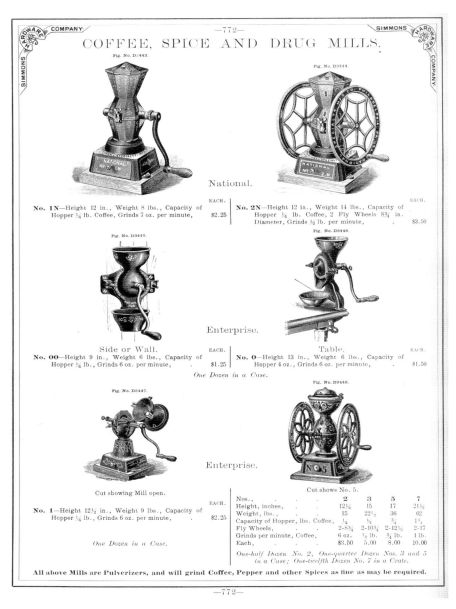

This page from the 1882 Simmons Hardware Company catalogue displays a selection of coffee and spice mills. *Missouri Historical Society, St. Louis.*

Above: The Simmons Hardware Company as seen from Eighth and Spruce Streets. The photo dates to 1900. *Missouri Historical Society, St. Louis*.

Right: A granitewear coffeepot from 1885 manufactured by St. Louis Stamping Company, with pewter trim added by Manning, Bowman and Company. *Missouri Historical Society, St. Louis*.

moderate taxes and other operating costs—the brothers invested in 3,500 acres in Madison County, Illinois. The new city created for the brothers' enterprise was named Granite City in honor of graniteware. In 1899, the Niedringhaus companies combined with others that produced enameled iron and tin products across the country to form the National Enameling and Stamping Company. The headquarters was established in New York City, with Frederick Niedringhaus as president.

Top Off Your Cup: Coffee and the Civil War

Napoleon Bonaparte may have said an army marches on its stomach, but for soldiers mired in the Civil War, coffee also played a role. Union soldiers annually were given thirty-six pounds of coffee by the government. They often used the butt of their rifles to crush and grind the beans. Once ground, coffee was brewed in a camp coffee pot or even directly in a soldier's tin cup.

Edwin Forbes's scene of Civil War soldiers around a fire. On the 1876 print below the image are the words "coffee coolers." *Missouri Historical Society, St. Louis.*

Lieutenant Colonel Walter King (Fourth Missouri State Militia Cavalry) modified a rifle with a built-in grinder for coffee or grain. An inspection board made a report on January 6, 1865, concerning the modification, pointing out issues, including the addition of extra weight to a soldier's equipment and compatibility with newer rifle models. However, the board permitted King, son of former Missouri governor Austin A. King, to conduct a field trial, equipping one hundred men with the coffee mill rifle. It's not known if these trials happened, as King was mustered out on April 20, 1865. The "Coffee Mill Sharps carbine" remains one of the rarest guns in collectors' circles.

When the port of New Orleans was blocked, Southern soldiers had to find substitutes for coffee, including brewing drinks from acorns, chicory and sorghum. While there was no caffeine, the drinks warmed a cold and hungry soldier.

By the 1860s, coffee imports had reached 180 million pounds. After the war, the coffee trade exploded in St. Louis, with existing roasting companies building up their business and new firms incorporating. Inventors perfected roasting machines and introduced household items to consumers that made brewing coffee at home easier and resulted in a more consistent quality.

In St. Louis, the Missouri Civil War Museum (222 Worth Road) offers more than one thousand artifacts throughout several galleries. Located in the former Post Exchange building at Jefferson Barracks, a military post that dates to 1826, the museum opened in 2013 and can be visited Wednesday through Sunday. During the war, Jefferson Barracks was used as a recruitment center for the Union army. A military hospital that treated more than eighteen thousand Confederate and Union soldiers by the end of the war also was on the site. For more information, visit https://mcwm.org.

4

THE COFFEE CAPITAL

1900–1929

In 1800, the United States imported 9 million pounds of coffee; by 1900, that amount exploded to 750 million pounds. Trade relations were improving around the world, and the first International Coffee Conference was held in New York in 1902. St. Louis's coffee industry likewise was healthy. There were no fewer than fifteen coffee dealers and wholesalers in the city according to the 1900 edition of *Gould's Commercial Register*.

And the city's work to bring a world's fair was well underway. By March 1901, finances were raised—a combination of state, federal and private monies totaling $15 million—and civic supporters incorporated as the Louisiana Purchase Exposition Company, with former mayor David Francis as president. Directors included coffee men Cyrus F. Blanke, William J. Kinsella and Julius Schotten. The fair was instrumental in spreading St. Louis industry to Mexico and Latin America, according to a 1906 report by the Latin-American Club and Foreign Trade Association. St. Louis's coffee industry had everything to gain from a successful fair.

MEET ME AT THE FAIR

The statistics for the 1904 Louisiana Purchase Exposition, held in St. Louis from April 30 through December 1, are impressive: a 1,200-acre site within Forest Park; sixty-two exhibiting countries and forty-three of forty-five states; 19.7 million attendees; and 1,500 buildings, including several palaces dedicated to topics including art, electricity, machinery and agriculture.

For food lovers, the 1904 World's Fair probably exceeded their wildest dreams. From dozens of international cuisines to the mile-long Pike lined with restaurants, food concessions and amusements, fairgoers had a smorgasbord from which to choose. The fair popularized the ice cream cone, hot dog, hamburger, iced tea and other handheld foods previously thought to be consumed only by ill-bred people. Cotton candy (called fairy floss) debuted in St. Louis, as did puffed rice. Formal restaurants, including Lüchow-Faust World's Fair Restaurant on the Pike, also were popular. The fair's largest (three thousand seats) restaurant featured two dozen entrées, more than twenty vegetable sides and eleven desserts on a menu devised by St. Louis's legendary restauranteur Tony Faust and the Lüchow restaurant family from New York.

The local coffee companies cashed in on the fair's buzz, from stamping commemorative tins to creating special blends. Getting one's brand in front of millions of fairgoers was the endgame. The Steinwender-Stoffregen Company's Yale brand was recognized as the best coffee at the fair. The company, as well as Forbes Tea and Coffee Company, used the name and image of comic strip character Buster Brown to sell their coffee. Artist Richard Outcault sold licensing rights to more than two hundred companies to use Buster and his dog, Tige, to advertise a variety of products.

But C.F. Blanke and Company arguably had the most inventive ideas for selling its coffee at the fair.

In 1903, Blanke bought the historic log cabin known as "Hardscrabble," built by Ulysses S Grant in 1856. In 1891, the cabin was disassembled and relocated to Webster Groves, a suburb west of St. Louis, by real estate businessman Edward Joy, who wanted to protect the historic cabin from treasure hunters.

Joy must have found the offer of $8,000 for the cabin—more than $200,000 by today's standards—too good to pass up, so he sold it to Blanke. Part of the company's sweeping 1904 World's Fair advertising campaign, the cabin was relocated by Blanke to the fairgrounds in Forest Park near the Palace of Fine Arts. Fairgoers could tour the cabin for ten cents and enjoy lunch or a cup of the company's award-winning coffee or tea inside the pavilion next to the cabin.

A portrait of Cyrus F. Blanke, 1900. *Missouri Historical Society, St. Louis.*

After the fair, Blanke hoped the cabin could stay in Forest Park, but his company and city leaders couldn't come to terms regarding the historic structure's maintenance. In 1907, Blanke sold the cabin to beer baron August Busch Sr., who relocated it to his estate in south St. Louis County. Today, visitors to Grant's Farm can see the cabin and hear part of its history during the tram tour of the grounds.

But Grant's cabin wasn't the only advertising gimmick Blanke had up his sleeve.

Village Boy was a Thoroughbred horse Blanke debuted in 1894, thirty-nine years before the famous Anheuser-Busch Clydesdales showed up in St. Louis. The horse had gained a certain amount of fame. During a vice presidential campaign stop in St. Louis, Blanke offered Theodore Roosevelt his personal mount, Village Boy, for a recreational horseback ride and photo opportunity. In 1903, another notable, General Frederick Dent Grant, son of Ulysses S Grant, rode Village Boy in the St. Louis World's Fair Dedication Parade. Another parade later that year, however, turned out poorly for Blanke and his horse. On the way to the parade, the animal slipped, fell and pinned Blanke to the ground. Blanke's ankle recovered, but Village Boy's back injury never healed, and the animal was put down in 1905.

Blanke moved from saddle horses to promotional automobiles. He commissioned a forty-five-passenger vehicle be built for the 1904 World's Fair. Dubbed Blanke Coffee Automobile (the first of its kind, according to a promotional booklet the company produced for the fair), the vehicle chauffeured fairgoers from the coffee factory to the fairgrounds.

The presence of Blanke coffee and tea at the fair was solidified with two displays in the Palace of Agriculture that not only showed product but also offered demonstrations on how to make the perfect cup of coffee. As many as ten concession stands, including cafés on the Pike, were operated by Blanke's coffee company. To get his tea and coffee in the hands of more fair concessionaires, Blanke ordered 125,000 branded china cups and saucers and offered them to anybody who would sell his coffee or tea.

Another well-known culinary personality also wanted to teach people how to make proper coffee. Sarah Tyson Rorer, renowned cookbook author, created the *St. Louis World's Fair Souvenir Cook Book*. It sold for fifty cents a copy. There are brief recipes for iced coffee and frozen coffee custard in the book. She also shared how to brew a good cup of coffee for the twentieth-century homemaker. Rorer felt that one needed fresh cold water, quality coffee (no chicory) and a percolator.

One of the Blanke Coffee pavilions from the 1904 World's Fair. *Missouri Historical Society, St. Louis.*

St. Louis coffee men agreed with Rorer about the importance of the right coffee pot. A 1905 ad in the *St. Louis Republic* promoted Hanley and Kinsella's H&K Coffee Maker, which may have been a predecessor to today's V60 coffee pots. Inside three-pound cans of H&K Coffee were a packet of paper filters and a coupon entitling the bearer to purchase this "expensive French coffee making machine" for fifty cents. Blanke, who had designed a "sanitary ceramic" drip pot and a coffee urn, in December 1909 received a U.S. patent for his drip coffee maker. It was advertised and sold across the country as "the perfect coffee pot." It was endorsed by the National Coffee Roasters Association.

But a more important development that impacted the sale of coffee and protected consumers was the passage of the Pure Food and Drug Act of 1906. This was the first federal law to regulate food and drugs to combat "misbranding" and "adulteration" and eventually led to the creation of the Food and Drug Administration. Prior to the law, some coffee companies in St. Louis were adding chicory or even sawdust into packages labeled as "pure coffee" or labeled lesser-grade coffee as premium.

Companies Incorporate, Expand

By 1911, there were no less than twenty-five coffee wholesalers in St. Louis. The foundation that had been laid in the century before by pioneering coffee men resulted in significant fruits during this era. Existing companies expanded and new companies incorporated. This also was the decade in which St. Louis coffee merchants launched their own organization.

As early as 1900, St. Louis coffee men, including Robert M. Forbes, Julius Schotten and Robert Meyers, discussed over lunches their concerns about freight rates, food purity and business ethics. By 1906, seeds for forming an organization were being planted in St. Louis. As a result, the Traffic Association of St. Louis Coffee Importers, the country's first coffee organization, was formed in 1910 by ten coffee firms. It elected Robert Meyer, president of Meyer Brothers Coffee, its president. This entity worked to control pricing, quality and transportation costs. This group would become the National Coffee Roasters Traffic and Pure Food Association. An organizational meeting of twenty-six coffee roasting businesses in the Mississippi Valley was held in May 1911 at the Planters Hotel in St. Louis, at which time Schotten was elected president. In 1912, the organization's name was simplified to the National Coffee Roasters Association. After 1940, the name was shortened to the National Coffee Association, and it remains active today.

In 1919, Julius Schotten was hit by a car while trying to cross a street and died. Control of the company his father founded passed at his death to Schotten's two children, Zoe and Jerome. Jerome bought out his sister in 1925. However, Schotten's widow, Pauline, was named vice-president, a notable appointment as the first female executive in St. Louis's coffee industry.

Another St. Louis coffee company blazed a new trail in the city's business scene. In 1913, Hanley & Kinsella Coffee & Spice Company was the first local company to institute an eight-hour workday for its employees while maintaining pay grades. Previously, female employees worked nine hours a week; male employees worked ten hours. William J. Kinsella Jr., following the retirement of his father in 1911, assumed the reins as vice-president and general manager. His brother, Dalton, was treasurer. When their father died in 1918, William Kinsella Jr. assumed the president's chair at the company, and operations were moved to Choteau Avenue.

Additional coffee men passed away in this era, often passing the reigns of their businesses to male heirs. Julius Steinwender (Steinwender-Stoffregen

An employee of the Hanley & Kinsella Coffee & Spice Company, circa 1910 to 1914. *Missouri Historical Society, St. Louis.*

Coffee Company) died on June 4, 1912, in New York. David G. Evans died in 1916, and his son Gwynne assumed the role of president. The firm was incorporated, and the name was changed to David G. Evans Coffee Company in 1917. In December of that year, the company's building on North Second Street burned, destroying the third floor. No one was injured, but according to a report in the *St. Louis Post-Dispatch*, Gwynne Evans said the company lost $75,000 in inventory and $30,000 in equipment. The newspaper reported in February 1918 that the company secured another location on North Second Street, a five-story, fifty-thousand-square-foot building formerly used as a grocery. A month later, the company was advertising in local newspapers for "girls for labeling and filling spice and coffee" and offering "good wages" at the new factory.

Owners of Forbes Tea & Coffee had an unhappy Christmas in 1924 as a fire broke out on Christmas Eve at the plant on North Main Street, causing more than $100,000 in damages. The company relocated to Clark Avenue.

At the Nash-Smith Tea and Coffee Company, Michael Smith moved into the president's chair following the death of George Nash Sr. in 1909. His son

George A. Nash became vice-president. In 1919, Nash left the company and was replaced by Walter M. Smith.

The early 1900s welcomed new coffee companies, including one that remains in business today.

Most visitors to the St. Louis World's Fair left with memories, full bellies and a souvenir or two, but brothers J.P and James J. O'Connor came away with an idea for a company. The St. Louis brothers watched a demonstration of coffee being roasted with heat generated by natural gas (the latest method). They soon set up Ronnoco (O'Connor spelled backwards) Coffee Company and delivered their gas-roasted coffee beans to local hotels.

James J. O'Connor left the company in 1910 to start his own company, O'Connor Coffee. In 1919, Frank Guyol Sr. bought Ronnoco Coffee; his family owned the company for about ninety years.

Leaving an established coffee company to start one's own business was a common practice in the early twentieth century. Floyd E. Norwine, born in 1877 in Mineral Point, Missouri, moved to St. Louis to work as a bookkeeper for C.F. Blanke Coffee Company. From 1899 to 1908, he was secretary and manager at Meyer Brothers Coffee Company, leaving to start Norwine Coffee Company, a coffee, tea and spice import business with offices on North Second Street.

Ben H. Johnson and associates started the Johnson-Allen Coffee Company around 1908. The company, dealers in coffee and tea, had Gunpowder as its flagship tea brand and Log Cabin—packaged in a tin log cabin that later could be used as a toy dollhouse—its coffee brand. The company was bought out in 1923 by Norwine Coffee Company. Norwine brands included Dining Car, Red Mill, Sunshine, Banker and Winter Gold. By 1925, Norwine Coffee Company was selling to grocers in eleven states.

By 1920, St. Louis had developed into the largest inland coffee distributor in the country. Before the end of the decade, seventy-five roasters were doing business in the city. The St. Louis Chamber of Commerce reported that coffee roasters did an annual business of more than 750,000 bags of coffee valued at more than $20 million. U.S. coffee imports by June 1920 totaled 1.4 billion pounds with a value of approximately $311 million. For that same period, coffee consumption in the United States was more than 12 pounds annually per capita.

The country's largest mail-order coffee company, St. Louis's H.P. Coffee, shipped 17.5 million pounds of coffee to twenty-four states in 1919. In March 1920, H.P. Coffee bought Western Tea and Spice Company for $500,000, the *St. Louis Globe-Democrat* reported. Henry Petring Grocery

In this 1930 photograph by Richard Fuhrmann, the Norwine Coffee Company building is seen at Fourth and Clark. Originally, the company was located on North Second Street. *Missouri Historical Society, St. Louis.*

Company, founded in 1853, changed its name in 1907 to H.P. Coffee Company, which did an annual business of $5 million in mail-order sales of coffee, tea, spices and extracts, as well as baking powder and baking soda. Other companies, including Roth-Homemeyer Coffee, realized expansions. That company in 1905 purchased land on Clark Avenue for its new seven-story, $200,000 building.

COFFEE AND WORLD WAR I

As it did in the Civil War, coffee helped boost the morale of troops during World War I. The U.S. War Department went as far as establishing coffee roasting plants in France so that its soldiers could have fresh, hot coffee at the ready. And an invention perked up the personnel much quicker: instant coffee.

Stories differ as to who invented instant coffee—some point to a New Zealander in 1890, others to a Japanese chemist in 1901—but the first business to mass-produce instant coffee, in 1910, was the G. Washington

A photo by Robert John Walker captures a Red Cross volunteer serving coffee to World War I soldiers from the 314th Engineers, 89th Division. The men were on their way to New York. Walker, a St. Louisian, served in the 314th Engineers, and his photographic collection recorded their training, activities in France and Germany and the trip home on the USS *Montana*. *Missouri Historical Society, St. Louis.*

The interior of Tony Faust's restaurant in St. Louis. It's said that Cyrus F. Blanke got his idea for instant coffee while dining at the restaurant. *Missouri Historical Society, St. Louis.*

Coffee Refining Company of Brooklyn, New York. Competitors soon followed, and by 1917, the U.S. government was buying all the instant coffee it could lay its hands on.

C.F. Blanke and Company was one of the manufacturers selling instant coffee to the government. The idea that Cyrus Blanke could make instant coffee happened at Faust's restaurant in St. Louis. When a drop of liquid coffee spilled onto a plate with a piece of mince pie had come out of the oven, Blanke witnessed that the spot dried up immediately. On examination, Blanke discovered that the stain had become very fine powder; when a drop of water was added, it reconstituted into coffee. He sold the product through one of his other companies, St. Louis Soluble Tea and Coffee Company.

In 1917, the *Tea and Coffee Trade Journal* reported that the Blanke company received an order for 250,000 cans of its Faust Instant Coffee. Each can of "Faust U.S. Trench Coffee" could make one hundred cups. This, as well as another order received just a few weeks before, totaled 960,000 cups of coffee for U.S. troops.

Another St. Louis business, the Wrought Iron Range Company, did its part to help provide coffee to World War I troops. Established in 1881 by brothers Henry, William and Lucius Culver with a small factory on Ninth Street, the company grew to become the largest producer of stoves in the city. Its Home Comfort Stoves were highly prized. During the war, Wrought Iron Range manufactured copper coffee urns, as well as commercial stoves, to be used by the military.

TOP OFF YOUR CUP: BLANKE'S FOLLY

Cyrus F. Blanke was not only a coffee magnate and inventor but also a visionary. But one of his most ambitious projects never fully got off the ground.

In November 1901, Blanke's Friede-Blanke Aerial Globe Company purchased a 5.65-acre tract of land between Clayton and Oakland Avenues for $32,500. On this site, Blanke and his associates intended to build a "city in the clouds," a massive aerial globe. Imagined by designer Samuel Friede and engineer Albert Borden, the all-steel structure would stand 700 feet above the grove and accommodate up to thirty thousand people at a time, according to the prospectus advertised in the *St. Louis Post-Dispatch*. (By comparison, today's landmark Gateway Arch at the St. Louis riverfront towers 630 feet in the air.) Sixteen elevators carried guests to the tiered attractions, such as the suspended gardens, coliseum, music hall, moving café and, finally, the rooftop palm garden more than four hundred feet above the ground.

The plan was to have the impressive attraction funded and opened by the start of the 1904 World's Fair. Blanke's company proposed selling St. Louis residents stock in the aerial dome company, with $2 million noted as the initial offering ($1 per share), of which half would be sold to the public.

But the initial capital couldn't be raised, and although the city approved of the plan and granted the necessary permits, the glorious aerial globe was never built.

5

SHIFTS IN ST. LOUIS COFFEE

1930–1949

R ow after row of shacks made of scrap wood, cardboard and anything else that could be scavenged composed St. Louis's Hooverville, one of the largest settlements of people displaced by the Great Depression. Although Hoovervilles—named after President Herbert Hoover—were scattered across the country, St. Louis had one of the largest. More than five thousand people lived in several hundred shacks along the Mississippi River south of the MacArthur Bridge (known then as Municipal Bridge). There were four churches inside Hooverville, which had its own mayor, and even a "suburb" called Hoover Heights.

According to the Missouri Historical Society, the City of St. Louis allocated nearly $1.5 million in relief funds between 1930 and 1932, and several charitable organizations gave aid to the city's neediest citizens. One charity, known as the Welcome Inn, served meals to some four thousand people per day. Sometimes, jobs could be found for Hooverville residents in exchange for produce. The organization, founded in 1930 by Katherine Franciscus, continued after 1933 and distributed food, clothes, coal and toys to the city's unhoused population.

Hooverville was an example of how hard the Depression hit St. Louis, the seventh-largest city in the country (population 820,000). By the spring of 1933, the city's unemployment rate was over 33.0 percent, higher than the national average of 24.9 percent. Throughout the state, almost half of all industrial workers lost their jobs.

It's interesting that Cyrus F. Blanke in 1921 told the St. Louis Chamber of Commerce: "The coffee business is one business that is never affected to any great extent by depression nor booms. Coffee drinkers of this country will drink a certain amount of coffee, no less in hard times and no more in prosperous times, but in prosperous times the merchants buy more freely than they do in hard times. They hold back buying in hard times just as long as they can."

However, the late 1920s and early 1930s impacted St. Louis coffee companies. Some were sold, others closed and a handful of other companies experienced expansion.

The Steinwender-Stoffregen Coffee Company was bought by James H. Forbes Tea and Coffee Company in 1931 for an undisclosed amount. Charles Stoffregen, board chairman, died the year before at age seventy-nine. His obituary recorded that he had been working at his desk the day before. His brother and partner, Herman, died in 1905.

Meyer Brothers Coffee and Spice Company was bought in 1929 by David G. Evans Coffee Company, the makers of Old Judge coffee, a popular St. Louis brand. Robert Meyer, former president of the Meyer Brothers operation, died in 1930. Nash-Smith in 1936 got out of the coffee roasting business and sold off its equipment at auction.

The Biston Coffee Company, after losing a lawsuit for nearly $300,000, went out of business in 1931. Gustave M. Biston Jr. started the company with his brother Ferdinand in the early part of the twentieth century, possibly 1917. An article in a 1922 edition of the *St. Louis Star and Times* noted Biston to be among the foremost coffee and spice companies in the country, trading in states in the North, Midwest and South. The company was located at Seventh and Clark in downtown St. Louis. Its brands were Golden Grains, Radio and Peaberry coffee.

But by 1927 and 1928, Biston Coffee had run into hard financial times. After the company met with creditors (Forbes Tea and Coffee Company, Hard and Rand Inc. and C.D. Kenny Company), newspaper articles reported it was agreed that Biston would dissolve and pay its debts of $145,000 over five installments. However, Biston's creditors soon grew impatient for the money and, according to testimony, instituted bankruptcy action, which the federal courts dismissed in May 1930. In August 1930, Biston Coffee sued for actual and punitive damages totaling $299,731 but lost the case in June 1931.

Gustave and his family remained in St. Louis after his business closed; he died in 1955. Ferdinand moved to Arizona several years before the

The Steinwender-Stoffregen Coffee Company building. *Missouri Historical Society, St. Louis.*

lawsuit and subsequent loss of the coffee and spice company; he was at one time the company's secretary and treasurer. He passed away in Tucson, Arizona, in 1933.

Consolidation throughout the country's coffee industries was a consequence of the Great Depression, and regional companies struggled to retain their market share against the big brands. Some of these national brands, as noted in *Uncommon Grounds*, launched attack ads against competitors in the mid-1930s. This had an adverse effect on consumers.

Most coffee trade members wanted attack ads stopped, according to *Tea & Coffee Trade Journal*, noting that consumers were giving up coffee in favor of other beverages, especially soft drinks. *Business Week* in 1936 reported that Coca-Cola was becoming a popular breakfast drink in the South, and the morning meal of a doughnut and a cola was catching on as far north as New York. Coffee companies in the 1930s also had new federal guidelines to work within under the National Recovery Administration.

President Franklin D. Roosevelt's National Recovery Administration (NRA) was established in 1933 to combat cutthroat competition and encourage fair practices. Businesses that supported the agency's codes could display the "blue eagle insignia" on packages, in ads and in windows. In 1935, the agency alleged that the mail-order wholesaler H.P. Coffee Company in St. Louis was selling its coffee below cost, a violation of the coffee code. Although H.P. Coffee's president, William H. Petring, agreed to surrender the blue eagle insignia, he told the *St. Louis Post-Dispatch*: "Our prices are always above our costs, but they [NRA] insisted on our maintaining prices at a fictious high level. Consequently, we found it desirable to give up the blue eagle. The only alternative was robbing the consumer and penalizing small dealers." The NRA folded in 1935.

The incident didn't hamper business for the company, which was noted for its flagship Trumpet coffee brand. In April 1935, H.P. Coffee moved into the building on the corner of Broadway and Clark Avenue once occupied by Steinwender-Stoffregen. The move was to consolidate the wholesaler's two locations into the larger building. H.P. Coffee also produced the popular Kake Kan Koffee brand, notable for its almost four-inch-tall red and gold tin that could be used to bake a cake when emptied of coffee.

The Rose Coffee Company also saw growth in the 1930s. Founded in the early 1900s by Isaac Rose, its coffee initially was roasted at Evans or Forbes coffee plants. With a need for more space, Rose completed a new warehouse on Laclede Avenue in November 1932. A teenage Joe Charleville, Rose's stepson, went to work at the plant during summers

Portrait of Isaac Rose, founder of Rose Coffee Company. *Courtesy Charleville family.*

doing a variety of odd jobs. After graduating high school, Charleville went to work full time making coffee deliveries and collecting money. He'd later move into sales. Dave Charleville, Joe's grandson, said, "He was the best salesman. He knew everybody," adding that his granddad mentioned that keeping the business going during the Great Depression was tough.

Hanley & Kinsella was another coffee company on the move, leasing in 1933 a three-story building on the corner of Tower Grove and Vandeventer Avenues. According to a report in the *St. Louis Globe-Democrat*, the move in part was due to the new location's proximity to the Frisco Railroad.

In 1939, a lawsuit was filed against the company. A Chicago company, Swanson Brothers, alleged that Hanley & Kinsella owed it more than $8,000 for green coffee and that the company had incurred "indebtedness more than the value of its tangible property." Swanson Brothers also claimed that CEO Virgil P. Leahy, President William J. Kinsella, Jr. and his brother and secretary, Dalton Kinsella, were operating the company at a loss. In a statement to the newspaper, William Kinsella said he was surprised at the filing and that the company "is getting along all right," adding that the suit would be resisted. Hanley & Kinsella was sold in 1940, and the company was dissolved several years later. William Kinsella died in 1954.

Radio Advertising

Clearly, retaining market share amid encroaching national brands and government regulations made the 1930s a challenging decade for local coffee companies. But coffee now had a powerful advertising ally—radio—and St. Louis businesses got creative.

In the mid-1930s, the David G. Evans Company partnered with KMOX radio for "Curious Questions," which promoted the Old Judge coffee brand. Listeners wrote and mailed in a curious question with the documented answer and, if applicable, a coupon inside a can of Old Judge coffee. Judges selected the questions to be read on the air, and cash prizes were awarded (triple the prize with the coffee coupon.)

James H. Forbes Tea and Coffee Company used KXOK radio announcer Bob Hillie to host the Forbes Food Store Quiz, staged in local grocers and retail stores selling Forbes' Culture Ripened or Martha Washington brands. Hillie interviewed shoppers, and the recorded conversations were used on the air. The contestants won prizes ranging from five dollars to a pound of Forbes coffee.

Manhattan Coffee, a General Grocer Company brand based in St. Louis, followed a robust print campaign with its own KXOK quiz show featuring announcer Don Phillips. The spots were peppered with the message, "Manhattan coffee / something different / not just as good." Manhattan Coffee increased sales by 30 percent.

Another Manhattan radio campaign involved more than 75 percent of St. Louis schools. During the radio program *Front Page Patrol*, the coffee roaster touted free uniforms for school safety patrol boys who could accumulate the required "votes," which really were proofs of purchase. In the 1940s, Manhattan advertised on a national radio program from Hollywood,

California, *I Want a Divorce*, offering a premium of six gold-trimmed glasses with proof of purchase of six pounds of coffee.

Some of Manhattan's most creative ad campaigns didn't involve radio or print media.

In the 1930s and 1940s, the Food Craft Shop occupied a floor at a large office building at 1124 Locust Street. It was a social space for the city's women's organizations, and its restaurant was noted for fine food service. Following a delightful lunch, the ladies participated in fifteen-minute presentations by the food companies and home-product suppliers financing the operation. Companies could provide the table linens or bridge score cards, but Manhattan managed to provide the ladies' coffee. In one year, thirty-five thousand cups of Manhattan coffee were served in branded china at the Food Craft Shop. Conveniently, a registration card was placed near the cup and saucer, giving the women a chance to submit their names, the name of the grocer they shopped at and whether they'd like to sample tea or coffee. The cards were collected, and promissory orders were filled and delivered to the grocer named on the card. Follow-up mailings to homes—fifty thousand in the first decade of the program—were made.

THE WAR YEARS

On June 19, 1942, the pioneering coffee man Cyrus F. Blanke died at the age of eighty. In January, Blanke fell while leaving a downtown bank and was trapped in a revolving door. He never recovered from the accident. His coffee business, C.F. Blanke Coffee and Products Company, once one of the largest in the city, shut down shortly after his death.

That same year, a twenty-four-year-old Frank J. Guyol Jr. left his family's business, Ronnoco Coffee Company, to enlist in the U.S. Army and served in the Philippines. He returned in 1946 and continued his long coffee career that would span seventy-five years. His father, Frank J. Guyol Sr., was president until 1956 and then served as chairman of the board. Ronnoco, a wholesale roaster, sold its coffee to restaurants, hospitals and other institutions. In 1937, the senior Guyol told a *St. Louis Globe-Democrat* reporter that in the catering business, coffee can make or break a meal, and while many catering managers know this, few give the proper care and attention to making a good cup of coffee.

As part of the bigger coffee picture, the per capita coffee consumption in the United States in 1941 had risen to sixteen and a half pounds, a new

The C.F. Blanke Tea and Coffee Company, located on South Seventh Street, 1910. The business closed in 1942. *Missouri Historical Society, St. Louis.*

record. Thanks in part to a coffee agreement the United States brokered with Latin American countries, relations with nations such as Brazil and Colombia were solid.

Then Japan attacked Pearl Harbor. America was once again at war.

The Office of Price Administration (OPA) froze coffee prices at their December 8, 1941 level. The U.S. Army requisitioned ten times as many bags of coffee a month, translating for the military to more than thirty pounds per capita.

Problems in getting green coffee beans from Latin America to the United States arose due to the limited shipping space, and by April 1942, coffee roasters had to cut production to 75 percent of the previous year's deliveries. That summer, the National Coffee Department of Brazil and the Quartermaster Corps of the U.S. Army sponsored a tour of Ida Bailey Allen—a cookbook author and home economist—to "army bakers' and cooks' schools and camps." In June 1942, she reached Jefferson Barracks in St. Louis, where she declared there was no coffee shortage. "We may be a little short on coffee, meaning we have to use it carefully, but that is far from being a condition of shortage," she told reporters.

Mess sergeants asked Allen questions about what to do with leftover coffee and how to make good coffee with chlorinated water. She told the men not to let coffee stand in metal containers but instead reheat coffee in nonmetal double boilers, although reheated coffee won't be as good as when it is freshly brewed. She also advised that they boil water for fifteen minutes before making coffee.

By September, coffee production was cut to 65 percent, and OPA announced that coffee rationing for civilians soon would begin. On October 26, 1942, OPA announced that beginning on November 28, coffee would be rationed to one pound per person every five weeks (about one cup a day). Not surprisingly, the National Coffee Association (NCA), which started in St. Louis about thirty years before, had something to say about this.

William Williamson, manager of the association, told United Press that rationing could have been avoided had it not been for a blundering War Production Board (WPB). "The WPB has treated coffee as a stepchild," he said. "It's not a lack of shipping space which has caused the present shortage but a lack of foresight on the part of some blundering people in WPB." Williamson maintained that the board had allowed ships to return from Central and South America with unused and improperly allocated cargo space and failed to recognize the value of coffee to civilian morale.

American coffee drinkers had to learn how to do more with less. For example, Blanche Gordon Wilson, a Springfield, Illinois resident and reader of the *St. Louis Post-Dispatch*, wrote to the newspaper, saying she had learned to make the same amount of coffee in the morning, but for dinner, fresh water was added to the used coffee grounds and percolated "a little longer." While a connoisseur may frown at her method, she wrote, "But in war time, which would one prefer to be, a connoisseur or a patriot?"

Some people resorted to creating beverages that resembled coffee using ingredients like yams and grain. A story from Atlanta, Georgia, picked up by the *St. Louis Star and Times* in 1942 describes roasting shredded yams mixed with grain and crushing the mixture into grounds that could be boiled with four cups of water.

But coffee rationing was short-lived. President Franklin D. Roosevelt announced the end on July 28, 1943, adding that sugar allowances would be increased soon. The following day, Gwynne Evans, vice-president of the NCA and president of David G. Evans Coffee Company, told the *Post-Dispatch* that the end of coffee rationing should put the coffee business "on a normal basis throughout the country."

In 1944, thirty-nine-year-old Dana Brown moved from Topeka, Kansas, to St. Louis to run the coffee department for General Grocer Company. Manhattan Coffee was the company's major brand. Within five years, Brown, who'd had success selling for the Fuller Brush Company and the Woolson Spice Company of Ohio, bought Manhattan Coffee. Over the next three decades, Brown built a legacy in the coffee business and a lasting imprint on his adopted city.

TOP OFF YOUR CUP: ST. LOUIS UNION STATION

It's a remarkable statistic: one hundred thousand people a day came through St. Louis Union Station at the height of World War II. But to Amanda Clark, it's more than numbers.

Clark is the community tours manager for the Missouri Historical Society and is well versed on Union Station history, including the years when the Union Station Canteen operated. St. Louis's historic train depot (built in 1894), perhaps more than anything, was a place where emotional exchanges happened between people, producing an untold number of hellos and goodbyes. But during war, those goodbyes weighed so much more.

"I think of the men from small towns in the Midwest who had never seen a big city, all from different backgrounds, and now they've all gathered together to head off into the next thing. It's very emotional," she said.

The Union Station Canteen welcomed servicemen and women from the early 1900s through 1981. *Missouri Historical Society, St. Louis.*

The canteen, which was operated by the USO during World War II, provided hospitality by way of free coffee, sandwiches and light refreshments. From 1942 to 1946, the canteen served four million servicemen and women in St. Louis on their way to assigned posts or overseas. During the time of great uncertainty, Clark can't help but think what a warm cup of coffee might have meant to them.

"Coffee has connections for people; it brought comfort, maybe a taste of home or a familiarity and a reason to chat with the person next to them," she said.

During Thanksgiving, the canteen provided free turkey sandwiches and trimmings plus a meal ticket to eat at a Union Station restaurant, according to an article in a 1943 edition of the *St. Louis Globe Democrat.* The station had a coffee shop that served soups, chili, hot or cold sandwiches, salads and desserts, as well as Fred Harvey's restaurant, complete with the famous Harvey Girls as servers.

St. Louis Union Station saw its heaviest traffic during World War II, as well as in 1904, the year of the Louisiana Purchase Expedition.

Although the USO operated the canteen during World War I, it was run by Red Cross workers and other local charities, including the YMCA and Women of the Knights of Columbus. An amusing article in the *St. Louis Globe-Democrat* in 1919 told of an army private passing through Union Station who showed off a bottle of dead cooties to canteen workers. Having contracted the biting parasites while serving in France, Arthur Wittbrodt (Third Battalion, 138th Division, Company K) told the Red Cross workers and others at the canteen that "bringing home a few prisoners of war of a different sort from the Germans might be worthwhile, so I saved them."

In 1978, the last passenger train rolled out of the station. The Union Station Canteen operated until 1981; the USO now operates canteens at Terminal One and Terminal Two inside St. Louis Lambert International Airport.

Today, Union Station (stlouisunionstation.com) is a popular St. Louis attraction that's home to the St. Louis Aquarium, the St. Louis Wheel and other amusements and restaurants, plus the five-hundred-room St. Louis Union Station Hotel. Catch an indoor light show inside architect Theodore Link's magnificent Grand Hall, which features an ornate, sixty-five-foot barrel-vaulted ceiling. On the second floor, the 1894 Café occupies the former Union Station Canteen space. While the Harvey Girls are gone, the space Fred Harvey's restaurant once occupied is now known as the Station Grille. When you take away a cup of coffee from the café or enjoy a meal at a restaurant, think about the thousands of servicemen and women who may have experienced a little comfort at Union Station.

6

COFFEE AFTER WORLD WAR II

1950–1979

In the 1950s, the St. Louis Cardinals played at Sportsman's Park under new corporate ownership, Anheuser-Busch, while the Browns left the city for Baltimore, Maryland, and became the Orioles. The "Father of Rock 'n' Roll," Chuck Berry, duckwalked across the stage to "Maybelline," and the "King," Elvis Presley, shook up Kiel Auditorium. Pork steaks sizzled on the grill at backyard barbecues, and dinner parties were capped with pots of mediocre percolated coffee.

American coffee by the end of World War II was anything but "all shook up." As described in *Uncommon Grounds*, it had become a standardized product made with average Brazilian beans that tasted nearly the same between brands. Food writer M.F.K. Fisher in 1945 wrote that coffee "comes in uniform jars, which we buy loyally according to which radio program hires the best writers." And she was right.

Global coffee prices after controls were lifted by the U.S. government in 1946 rose steadily and by 1947 reached 50¢ per pound. For the first time, global coffee imports reached $1 billion.

Businesses passed on the increased cost of green beans. That five-cent cup of coffee at the neighborhood diner jumped to seven or ten cents per cup, while some coffee companies advertised (whether true or not) that their brand took fewer grounds to make a strong cup. Old Judge Food Corporation (formerly the David G. Evans Coffee Company), which was producing three million pounds of coffee a month, advertised that its

Old Judge brand was "irradiated," a technology that exposed the green coffee beans to high ultraviolet levels to kill microorganisms and improve the coffee's flavor; the latter claim, however, was difficult to prove.

Although it had been around since World War I, instant coffee's popularity exploded after World War II. By 1952, instant coffee accounted for 17 percent of coffee consumption in the United States. It seemed the postwar consumer was more interested in convenience than flavor.

Still, an interesting new era was emerging in St. Louis's coffee industry. More consolidation, including those of a few big names, took place. Coffeehouses were added to the entertainment district known as Gaslight Square. Inventive advertising and public relations campaigns emerged to promote brands, producing some of the city's classic media moments. And a new coffee mogul emerged literally from the bush to create one of the city's most iconic brands.

Pitching the Perfect Cup

Advertising gimmicks were nothing new to St. Louis coffee businesses, but now the magnates had television at their disposal.

Old Judge used a magician in a tuxedo and bow tie in early television spots. Standing in front of a curtain flanked by two Old Judge coffee signs, the pitchman started with "Hello, there. I'm the Old Judge Coffee Magician," followed by a simple magic trick using a large deck of cards, a rope or a scarf. After the quick demonstration, the slogan "But there's no trick to making a good cup of coffee" introduced the different coffee grinds to viewers. The commercials also mentioned that one pound of Old Judge could make eighty, ninety or one hundred cups of coffee "should you wish to stretch your coffee budget" while still retaining the "distinctive Old Judge flavor."

James J. O'Connor Coffee Company showcased St. Louis–area hotels that served its coffee in a series of television ads. Instead of entertaining viewers with magic or skits, O'Connor presented brief histories of hotels while cutting in shots of dining rooms or coffee shops within the hotel. Hotel publicity departments often helped with the research, and the commercials always included signs reading "O'Connor Coffee Served with Pride."

More Consolidation

James J. O'Connor was busy buying smaller coffee businesses. In May 1951, O'Connor bought the Hicks-Jensen Coffee Company as part of an expansion to service more restaurants, hotels, schools and other institutions. The firm in 1962 purchased the George Cousins Tea & Coffee Company, which continued operating under the same name as a division of O'Connor Coffee's restaurant division. In 1964, Pontiac Tea and Coffee Company was bought out by O'Connor for an undisclosed amount of cash. The company had been in business since the 1920s and serviced restaurants and hotels. Its employees were added to O'Connor's company payroll.

John P. O'Connor, owner of J.P. O'Connor grocery and, with brother James J., founder of Ronnoco Coffee Company, passed away in August 1951 at the age of eighty-seven. James J. O'Connor died in September 1968 at the age of eighty-five.

One of the first coffee companies in St. Louis, James H. Forbes Tea and Coffee, in February 1956 was bought for $750,000 by the H.B. American Machine Company of Chicago, which sold it a few months later to Woolson Spice Company of Toledo, Ohio. The year before, Forbes had recorded $6 million in sales, the majority coming from coffee.

Charles Forbes, great-grandson of the company's founder, said his father, James, was president at the time of the sale. Charles has a website (forbescoffee.org) devoted to Forbes coffee history. He said the Forbes coffee building at 922 Spruce Street was not part of the sale. August "Gussie" Busch Jr. in the 1960s had plans to build Busch Memorial Stadium downtown and wanted good access to the ballpark, which opened in 1966. The Forbes family sold the building to make way for a highway ramp, but a former employee saved a couple of bricks from the coffee building as it was being torn down. Charles said he's still got one of them. Interestingly, Forbes supplied roasted peanuts (a sideline for the company) to Sportsman's Park, former home of the Cardinals and St. Louis Browns, for a short period of time.

Manhattan Coffee in 1959 was sold to Cain's Coffee of Oklahoma City. Manhattan, thanks to its aggressive advertising and PR campaigns in the 1930s and 1940s, had developed a strong presence in the market. After World War II, it expanded its trade and private label business and in 1958 modernized its roasting plant. Now with its unification to Cain's, the Oklahoma coffee company was one of the largest roasting enterprises in the United States.

A female worker in 1955 at the Old Judge Coffee plant on North Second Street watches as a machine fills cans with coffee. *Missouri Historical Society, St. Louis.*

A brand known to St. Louis for nearly one hundred years, Old Judge Food Corporation in June 1957 was sold to Shaffer Stores and R.C. Williams and Company, food processors and distributors based in New York City. The sale was largely one in terms of management; Old Judge continued to be sold and headquartered in St. Louis. Joe G. Wick, president and treasurer, resigned, as did James McClellan, general counsel. Wick started in 1939 with the company when it was known as David G. Evans Coffee Company, working up from sales to the president's office. In 1964, the New York–based Chock full o' Nuts Corporation bought the Old Judge brand, which was sold through the 1980s.

Consolidations and mergers also affected smaller companies that concentrated on serving local coffee drinkers.

Since 1893, the J. Vaughan Coffee Company had sold coffee, tea and spices in downtown St. Louis. It was originally a wholesale business, but founder John W. Vaughan in 1903 switched to selling to individuals, first from a stall at the old Union Market and then from a shop on St. Charles Street.

Vaughan's son John C. at age fifteen started behind the counter at his dad's shop and remained in the store for more than fifty years, selling coffee much like shopkeepers in the century before did. Customers came into Vaughan's and purchased coffee by the pound, weighed on an old scale and put into paper bags. John C. Vaughan in 1967—a few months before he closed the business—told the *St. Louis Post-Dispatch* that consumers no longer seemed interested in the type of coffee bean but rather purchased by brand.

Vaughan bought green coffee from Colombia and Brazil and then paid a local roaster two cents a pound to roast and deliver the beans to his store. For his discerning customers, Vaughan created special blends just for them. Although the busiest time for his family's business was right after World War II, business had steadily dropped since the mid-1950s.

Another company with a local focus, Rose Coffee, realized an uptick in business in the 1950s. Dave Charleville Jr., grandson of owner Joe Charleville, said the company weathered the Great Depression and war rationing to reap rewards servicing their clients of St. Louis restaurants, clubs, hotels, hospitals and other institutions. Joe's sons, David and Tom Charleville, worked alongside their father until David left to open a specialty coffee café. After touring Europe to learn everything he could about espresso, he opened Coffee Charleville in 1973 in the affluent St. Louis suburb of Frontenac.

"It did OK but not good enough, and he ended up at Rose," said his son Dave Charleville.

In 1976, David left the family's coffee business, moved with his wife and two sons to Laramie, Wyoming, and opened an office supply store (although he later returned to St. Louis and to coffee).

When Joe sold Rose Coffee to Ronnoco in 1977, he told *St. Louis Commerce* magazine that coffee is a dying business being taken over by giants. He died on March 16, 2011.

In 1964, Ronnoco Coffee continued acquiring smaller companies with its purchase of Demmas Coffee (Mike Demmas, president), located on Hampton Avenue, for an undisclosed amount of money. An article in the *Post-Dispatch* noted that Ronnoco was St. Louis's largest wholesale coffee company.

Ronnoco's president, Frank J. Guyol Jr., in March 1964 created Dine-Mor Foods Inc. with partners from Denver, Colorado, and Kansas City, Missouri. It was an institutional coffee company that sold to national accounts across the United States. By 1969, Ronnoco was roasting six million pounds of coffee a year at its location on Dodier Street for its hotel, restaurant (including eight Pope's Cafeteria locations and Seven Kitchens and Round Table

Restaurants) and institutional clients. Frank J. Guyol, Ronnoco's chairman, died on February 5, 1970, at the age of eighty-five; sons Frank and William continued operating the company.

SAFARI COFFEE

Dana Brown with his Safari brand of coffee. *Courtesy Dana Brown Charitable Trust.*

"This is safari land, and I'm Dana Brown."

Anyone living in the St. Louis area in the 1960s and through the 1980s remembers that line from the ubiquitous television commercials for Safari Coffee featuring the company's unconventional owner, Dana Brown. A complex man who was born in 1905 in West Virginia, Brown grew up in poverty and left home at fourteen years of age. Working in lumber camps and on construction sites, he eventually landed a sales job with the Fuller Brush Company in Ohio and was a manager within six months.

His talent for sales brought him in the mid-1940s to the General Grocer Company to take charge of the coffee operation. Within five years, he'd worked his way to the president's position. Brown, an avid big-game hunter, used his safaris to tell how coffee was sourced, and the experiences were used in 1950s advertising.

But Manhattan's new ownership wasn't keen on supporting Brown's expensive African treks and refused to pay for the travel. He filed a lawsuit but lost, and in 1966, Brown left Manhattan Coffee to start his own company, Dana Brown Private Brands. (A later appeal was ruled in Brown's favor.)

Brown was a shrewd and clever marketer, and his underlying message with his safari commercials was that the consumer opens an adventure when they open a can of his coffee—even though it was quite like the other locally roasted brands. The television ads, however, were anything but mediocre.

The spots always started with a "slice of life" while on safari with Brown. There were shots of treks or of Brown holding an exotic animal while he explained something about the beast. Some of the animals handled by Brown were from a zoo in Africa he frequently visited. If the audience liked Brown's tales from Africa, it was an easy step to believe him when he gave the sales pitch about how great Safari Coffee tasted. One of the commercials featured a camp cook grilling buffalo liver over hot coals while Brown explained how delicious the delicacy was, especially when served with Dana Brown Safari Coffee.

Although his camps were costly (the safaris, which often included thirty men, cost upward of $30,000 each), the commercials helped Brown amass a fortune of $40 million in twenty years. And when he wasn't hunting on safari, he was in St. Louis pushing his coffee. Brown is described in a 2010 documentary by St. Louis's HEC-TV as a lifelong bachelor who ate out for dinner every night with friends. Yet this big-game hunter who decorated his apartment, office and car with animal skins and trophies wrote poetry and donated money to many St. Louis charities and institutions. An extensive list is found at his charitable trust's website, danabrowncharitabletrust.org.

Brown maintained that hunting and conservation could coexist in Africa if the animal wasn't on an endangered list. His friends have said that he gave meat from his kills to villages, although he eventually switched from guns to cameras on his safaris.

Brown died at age eighty-nine on October 21, 1994. His company was dissolved in 1996, but his charitable trust continues to serve his adopted city of St. Louis.

Gaslight Square's Coffeehouses

While known for its nightclubs and restaurants, Gaslight Square, at the intersection of Olive Boulevard and Boyle Avenue, also featured a handful of colorful coffeehouses, including Montileone's, the Laughing Buddha, the Exit, Insomniac, the Other Side and Chez Café. The coffeehouses, like their predecessors in the prior century, offered patrons stimulating conversation over steaming cups of coffee. But the twentieth-century iterations also included live music and light fare. These establishments, already in the "bohemian" part of the city, no doubt were filled with talk about the war in Vietnam, the civil rights movement and current events in St. Louis.

At Montileone's (4237 Olive), owner Ralph Montileone infused his knowledge of antiques with a desire to open in 1960 an espresso café in a beautiful old home. With the help of partners Sam Clark and Bob Powers, the space was renovated to exude "Venetian elegance" with "old Vandeventer Place overtones," as described in the *Globe-Democrat*. The espresso machine Montileone purchased in Milan, Italy, produced coffee that was "never more than five minutes from the beans," he told the newspaper.

Above: A couple in the 1960s enjoys coffee at Montileone's, located in popular Gaslight Square. *Missouri Historical Society, St. Louis.*

Left: The exterior of Montileone's coffee shop in Gaslight Square. *Missouri Historical Society, St. Louis.*

The Laughing Buddha opened in April 1960 inside the Musical Arts Building, which dated to 1904. For his website, Lost Tables (losttables. com), Dr. Harley Hammerman visited with the former owner, Lee Young. According to Hammerman, the Laughing Buddha didn't serve alcohol but offered a variety of coffee drinks (coffee purchased from the local O'Connor Coffee Company), teas and Lee's favorite, hot chocolate. Ciders and imported soft drinks were served, along with pastries from a local bakery and simple sandwiches.

Popular with the underage crowd, the Laughing Buddha also booked national folk musicians, including Judy Collins and Peter Yarrow (of Peter, Paul and Mary fame). But a fire on January 10, 1962, did significant damage to the historic Musical Arts Building, and the Laughing Buddha closed.

A Christian coffeehouse, the Exit, opened at 444 Boyle Avenue on October 1, 1964. According to an article in the *Post-Dispatch*, organizers wanted a relaxing space for "meaningful discussion" and folk music amid the revelry found at Gaslight Square. At the Other Side (4210 Olive Street), jazz and poetry were offered with espresso and coffee drinks.

By the mid-1960s, discos and burlesque houses helped attract crowds more intent on raising a little hell than enjoying classic jazz. The iconic gaslights were turned off (bills weren't paid), the old clubs closed and the Exit was shuttered in May 1969. By 1972, the once-vibrant Gaslight Square glowed no more.

Top Off Your Cup: Gaslight Square

What was the impetus behind the growth and popularity of St. Louis's once-thriving entertainment district? Interestingly, a catastrophic tornado fueled the rise of Gaslight Square.

On February 10, 1959, a tornado (an unusual weather occurrence for a St. Louis winter) ripped through the center of town, including Gaslight Square, which had been since the 1950s a funky little area known as Greenwich Corners populated with antiques shops and hangouts mainly for beatniks and other bohemians. Most of the city didn't know much about the area.

But after the tornado, "sightseers" came to witness the damage and insurance adjusters showed up with their checkbooks, creating the perfect storm for urban development. In less than a year, the district (now called Gaslight Square) was jammed with clubs, restaurants and coffeehouses. The university set mingled with the beatniks, and men in suits and women in flouncy attire filled the outdoor spaces. National talent (including Barbra Streisand, the Smothers Brothers, Miles Davis and Woody Allen) showed up to perform. Gaslight Square became the place to be in St. Louis.

The story of Gaslight Square shifted on December 30, 1964, when Lillian Heller, a local artist, was killed in the vestibule of her apartment building within the district. Shop owners started locking doors during the day. Discos and strip joints took over spaces once occupied by businesses that already moved out of the area. Thieves preyed on crowds, and despite the police providing added patrols, crime continued.

Hammerman noted in an article about several Gaslight Square establishments that many opinions and theories have been circulated regarding the demise of the once-vibrant entertainment district. "Some believe its very success is what killed it," wrote Hammerman. "The charm of the original square evaporated into noisy and rowdy crowds. Crime was also a factor in the decline."

In 1972, O'Connell's pub, the last "Gaslighter," relocated from Boyle Avenue to Kingshighway Boulevard, and later that year, the St. Louis Board of Aldermen put the final nail in the square's coffin, restoring the storied strip as a part of Olive Boulevard.

7
ST. LOUIS COFFEE

1980 to Today

The sun had been up only about an hour on the morning of the Thirteenth Annual Maplewood Coffee Crawl, and people were already in the check-in line to collect their mug and ticket. It was a chilly March morning with gray skies, but the prospect of tasting some of St. Louis's best coffee kept the crowd in a convivial mood.

Event organizers were expecting about 950 people throughout the morning, which was divided into two segments, each featuring different coffee roasters and shops. Throughout the morning, tasting lines grew longer, but since I was part of the "early risers group," the wait times weren't bad. Walking up to the tasting table at Living Room Coffee and Kitchen, I received a small cup of single-origin Guatemalan cold brew with house-made rosemary syrup, which was a pleasant surprise. I stopped at Kakao Chocolate to taste the award-winning Viennese truffle infused with coffee by Stringbean Coffee Company's Redeye Roast before heading to the remaining four stops on my segment of the crawl, the region's first and only walkable tour of caffeine, according to the City of Maplewood.

The coffee crawl is an illustration of the passion to be found today in St. Louis among its coffee roasters and sellers. It's all here, from large companies like Ronnoco to micro-roasters that amass a loyal following. If you love coffee, St. Louis is your kind of city. Let's meet some of the people who are passionate about producing outstanding coffee. We'll begin with a list of St. Louis City and County roasteries with their own coffee bar or café.

BLUEPRINT COFFEE

At Blueprint Coffee on Delmar Boulevard, espresso, vanilla cream and carbonated seltzer are ingredients in the Italian Espressoda. *Deborah Reinhardt.*

The American Planning Association named the Delmar Loop one of the ten greatest streets in America, a fact St. Louisans have known for a long time. A hundred years ago, this stretch of the city was called "the Loop" because of the westbound streetcars that "looped around" before connecting to other routes. Today, the Delmar Loop stretches for eight blocks and is filled with wonderful restaurants, shops, galleries and entertainment venues. And coffee lovers know that the Delmar Loop has been home to Blueprint Coffee (6225 Delmar Boulevard) for nearly ten years.

There's always a steady flow of pedestrian and vehicular traffic along this stretch of Delmar Boulevard. People are constantly coming and going. But on a recent visit to Blueprint Coffee, it seemed a good idea to sip an Italian Espressoda outside at one of the street tables and watch the world go by. Savoring the delicious mixture of vanilla syrup, soda water, cream and a double shot of Penrose (the house espresso) while people-watching felt, well, "Italian" and just right for a warm spring afternoon. Folks in business casual dress and workout clothes breezed in and out of Blueprint. Making great coffee available to everyone is the company's mission.

Blueprint was started in 2013 by six "members" (founders), five of whom had worked for Kaldi's Coffee. Nora Brady, Mike Marquard, Mazi Razani, Kevin Reddy and Andrew Timko came to coffee from diverse backgrounds, but all found gratification behind the coffee bar. Brian Levine returned to St. Louis and found that he and his wife missed the coffee experiences they had enjoyed on the West Coast. Friends connected them with the members, who were talking about starting Blueprint, and he was in.

While their stories vary, everybody involved with Blueprint is serious about coffee, and that's probably an understatement. From cultivating long-lasting relationships with the farmers in Central and South America with whom they deal directly, to providing in-depth classes to help baristas (and any coffee-obsessed people who can keep up), Blueprint dives deep into the world of coffee. The website (blueprintcoffee.com) also has helpful steps for making a great cup of coffee at home.

In addition to the coffee bar and roastery on Delmar, Blueprint has a location on Watson in the Lindenwood Park neighborhood and provides coffee service at the High Low Coffee Bar downtown inside the Kranzberg Arts Foundation on Washington Avenue. Thanks to the wholesale side, shoppers can find Blueprint Coffee at Whole Foods markets, and several restaurants and coffee shops serve their coffee. At Blueprint, it's all about building relationships, one cup at a time.

Coffeestamp

Growing up in Honduras, brothers Patrick and Spencer Clapp know about good coffee. The brothers told *Feast* magazine that they had their first cup as young as twelve years. Family friends owned a coffee farm just a few hours from their home city of El Hatillo. The brothers' everyday coffee was created from locally grown and picked beans. It can't get fresher than that.

But work in Honduras was not easy to find, so in 2012, the brothers moved to the United States to work for an uncle, which eventually led to construction work in New Orleans and, finally, to St. Louis in 2016. They noticed a great difference in quality and price of coffee stateside versus coffee in Honduras. Patrick Clapp, general manager and head roaster, told *Feast* that he and his brother often said they should bring coffee from Finca la Alondra (their friends' coffee farm) to St. Louis. He and Spencer were already considering leaving construction to do something else, and they pushed ahead to roast Honduran coffee in St. Louis, even though plenty of folks told them there were too many roasters in town.

In 2018, they started a micro-roastery using direct-trade beans from Finca la Alondra after learning all they could about roasting coffee, and the following year, their product was available at Soulard Market. By 2020, they had secured a second-story building (2511 South Jefferson Avenue) in the Fox Park neighborhood and bought a commercial roaster. Their plan was to roast and hand-pack coffee on the second floor and offer a café on the first floor. Then COVID hit. Without the daytime construction work and their retail outlet at Soulard closed, the Clapps sold their coffee online through their website (coffeestamp.com). But the pause allowed the brothers to build their first-floor café. By August 2020, their patio was open, and they offered curbside service to customers.

As the business has grown, Coffeestamp, working with importers, now offers ethically sourced, single-origin, sustainable coffee from countries

Patrick (*left*) and Spencer Clapp, owners of Coffeestamp. *Courtesy Coffeestamp.*

including Mexico, Costa Rica and Colombia. Their Vector blend uses coffee from Brazil, Uganda and Zambia. The Clapps' coffee is available exclusively at their café and through their website, and Patrick Clapp said he roasts up to 1,200 pounds of coffee per month. Lighter roasts help bring out the flavor nuances of each coffee.

But one of their coffees has a special mission. Sales of Finca la Alondra Reserva will raise money to assist a school in Honduras. Patrick, who said his mother, older brother and "a lot of friends" remain in Honduras, will raise $2,500 from that micro-lot (about five hundred bags), which they will "match with out-of-pocket money" to install solar panels by November 2022 when the school is on break.

While projects and family in Honduras keep the brothers Clapp connected, the café's menu, overseen by kitchen manager Spencer Clapp, gives St. Louis a taste of Latin America. The establishment is noted for its Cubano and empanadas, and the menu includes burritos for breakfast and lunch, Mayan tortilla and coconut or turtle alfajores (a butter sandwich cookie that's popular throughout Latin America). Patrick said drinks and empanadas change according to season.

As its name implies, Coffeestamp can provide an exotic break to one's day. Without leaving St. Louis, one is connected to different countries through coffee and comforting foods.

Coma Coffee Roasters

When siblings Macy and Corbin Holtzman in 2016 opened Coma Coffee Roasters in the University Tower (1034 South Brentwood Boulevard), they knew it would fill a void of specialty coffee shops in the Brentwood area. As a centrally located suburb of St. Louis County, the area has hundreds of businesses.

But Coma Coffee's location in the University Tower is unique for two reasons. The Holtzmans' father, Douglas Holtzman, founder of the commercial real estate firm STLCRE (St. Louis Commercial Real Estate), owns the building. And this was the location of the now-defunct University Club.

Founded in 1872, the University Club was a private men's organization that served to connect college and university graduates. According to the University of Missouri–St. Louis's Mercantile Library, the club hosted lectures featuring dignitaries representing literature, science and art, including Charles Lindbergh. It wasn't until 1968 that women could become full members. In 1975, the club built the tower at the southeast corner of Clayton and Brentwood Boulevards. The University Club, which occupied the top three floors of the building, closed in 2007.

A vibrant coffee café made sense for the University Tower. Employees of the tower's various tenants make up the large part of Coma Coffee's regular customers, according to Randall Buchanan, Coma's wholesale and retail operations manager. And from the start, drum-roasting coffee in-house was part of their business plan.

"Macy had made the move very early on to roast all coffee in-house so that we could supply a product that we loved and had our hands on," Buchanan said. "Crafting the best cup has been a priority for Macy and Corbin at the very start."

Their beans are sourced from Latin America and Africa via importers and recently from Coma's first farm-direct source in Kenya.

"This is a very special coffee and allows for us to jump more into farm-direct coffees. More money goes to the farmer this way," Buchanan said, who managed several coffee bars prior to coming to Coma Coffee.

But a great cup of coffee to start your morning or revive your afternoon is only part of Coma's story. Head chef Miranda Mooney's full café menu starts with breakfast (from bagels to burritos, hash to loaded toast) and moves into lunch, offering items like the popular smash burger and grilled sandwiches, quesadillas and fresh salads. There's also a full bar, and from 4:00 to 6:00 p.m. Monday through Friday, Coma Coffee hosts a happy hour.

When the pandemic shut down office buildings and employees headed home to work, Buchanan said Macy Holtzman dove into action. Placing Coma Coffee on the various platforms that offered online food orders, she was among the staff who ran food to the curb for their guests. "That produced an increase in our sales," Buchanan said, adding that the continued business of their regular guests helped them survive those months.

The online orders were kept and remain popular with customers. Bags of coffee also can be purchased online (comacoffee.com) by the bag or through Coma's subscription service. And, Buchanan said, some area Walmart stores are expected to start carrying Coma Coffee through the Coffee Collective Company, a Bentonville, Arkansas–based business that partners with specialty coffee roasters in various markets.

KALDI'S COFFEE

People flowed in and out of Kaldi's café in the DeMun neighborhood (700 DeMun Avenue) as effortlessly as the coffee being poured inside. Some customers settled at tables in the back room, while others (including a businessman and a gentleman soaking up the spring sunshine with his dog) found a place at the street-side patio. Students with backpacks and women with posh purses ordered from the coffee bar.

Since 1994, Kaldi's location in the popular Clayton neighborhood just ten minutes west of downtown St. Louis has been a gathering spot. Today, with several cafés plus the roastery, Kaldi's has grown to be a vital part of the local coffee culture. But its story began with two St. Louis journalists, a prime piece of real estate and a yearning for great coffee.

Howard Lerner and Suzanne Langlois worked at the *St. Louis Business Journal* and were introduced to specialty coffee as students at the University of Missouri–Columbia's journalism school. Although Kansas City had a few coffee roasters and cafés, St. Louis was behind when it came to cool places to enjoy a great cup of coffee.

Then Lerner received a tip from a friend that a property (once a travel agency, then a meditation center) was on the market. He left the newspaper job in July 1994 and, with the help of Langlois's father, built the café, which opened in October 1994. They offered pastries and sourced their coffee from a Kansas City roaster. In 1995, the business partners bought their first coffee roasting machine. Over time, the roastery moved to Gratiot Street.

Kaldi's original café on DeMun Avenue in Clayton. *Deborah Reinhardt.*

Ownership changed in 2005 when the Zimmer family bought half the coffee company; the buyout was completed in 2007. Today, Don Zimmer and co-owners son, Tyler Zimmer, and daughter, Tricia Zimmer-Ferguson, remain involved in the expanding company.

Honolulu Coffee, owned by Kaldi's, has several cafés in Hawaii, and Kaldi's opened a roasting facility there a few years ago that also explains the history of coffee in the state. Kona, the only coffee grown in the United States, is roasted and featured there.

Kaldi's Coffee Roasting Company is also expanding in the southeastern part of the United States. Frank McGinty, director of marketing, said there are now five Kaldi's locations on the campus of Emory University in Atlanta, Georgia. Kaldi's also has a "licensed concept" at the Georgia Institute of Technology in Atlanta.

They've also entered a roasting partnership with Frothy Monkey, a Tennessee café and wholesale bakery chain that was one of Kaldi's wholesale coffee customers for several years. "Five or six years ago, they wanted to get into roasting coffee, so we started a joint venture," McGinty said, adding that Kaldi's is co-owner of the Frothy Monkey Coffee Roasting Company.

And more locations are coming to the St. Louis metro area, McGinty said. After opening the company's first drive-through location in Ellisville (a western suburb of St. Louis) in summer 2022, McGinty said another, in St. Charles, Missouri, is planned for early 2023.

"We've always thought about it, but during the pandemic, it made a lot of sense," he said. "People have changed their buying habits. Our mission is not to jeopardize any of the quality we offer in our walk-in cafés but offer it through a convenient drive-through model."

Kaldi's offers a variety of single-origin and blended coffees (kaldiscoffee. com), including their flagship blend, 700, named for the original café at 700 DeMun Avenue. There's also a Roaster's Choice subscription service that rotates a new coffee every calendar month. Subscribers can choose how often they want coffee shipped to their homes. Select coffees also are available at Schnucks markets.

In 2019, Kaldi's roasted one million pounds of coffee. "That was a cool benchmark for us," McGinty said. "We'll get back to that pretty quick."

LC COFFEE ROASTERS

Coffee can make a difference in people's lives. Just ask Jamie Jeschke, cofounder of LC Coffee Roasters (formerly La Cosecha Coffee Roasters) (7360 Manchester Road). As a college student in Springfield, Missouri, Jeschke said he got into coffee "mostly to stay awake." When he moved to St. Louis, he and his wife met John (Gio) Sparks and his wife at church and learned that Sparks was quite good at roasting coffee at home using air popcorn poppers.

"He shared it with me and that's how I got involved with it," Jeschke said. They shared their coffee with friends and family. Then, the attractive price of green coffee in the early 2000s, coupled with the realization of the plight of coffee farmers, fueled a decision to leave their jobs (Jeschke's background was in international sales; Sparks's was in IT) to start La Cosecha Coffee Roasters in 2006.

"We wanted to buy direct trade coffee so farmers would get a fair price," Jeschke said. "We also thought our name (Spanish for "the harvest") would be a good way to connect consumers with farmers. It described what our business was all about."

For the first six years, LC Coffee was roasting and selling coffee wholesale to a handful of local coffee bars, bakeries and grocers, including Global Foods. Jeschke said he delivered the coffee—air-roasted at the time—in small batches.

"The first six years we had an air roaster that could only do eight-pound batches. The more common is a drum roaster. Our Diedrich is made in Idaho. We can do up to twenty-five pounds at a time. We also have a little more control over our roasts, so that's why we switched."

Their sustainably grown and ethically sourced coffee comes from the Pacific Rim, Africa and Latin America. An opportunity came to open a coffee bar in Maplewood (a central suburb in St. Louis County), partnering with Great Harvest Bread Company, wholesale coffee customers. It was a logical next step, and the roastery was moved to that location. In 2013, a

LC Coffee Roasters in Maplewood focuses on its coffee. Great Harvest Bread Company, which shares the space, provides food service. *Deborah Reinhardt.*

third partner, Gregory Lowe, came on board to oversee the front of the house. Sparks eventually sold his share of the company.

When COVID hit, Jeschke said their online sales (lccoffeestl.com) took off, because people were making coffee at home instead of frequenting their favorite coffee bars. And in 2021, LC Coffee launched a coffee truck known affectionately as "Brewster" that brings coffee service to special events. It's also at the Kirkwood Farmers Market every Saturday, he said. "The coffee truck has also helped our retail sales," Jeschke said, adding that the business is about 70 percent retail, 30 percent wholesale.

When asked if the Maplewood location, which is home to other roasters and coffee cafés, helps or hurts his business, Jeschke acknowledged that the community "is saturated, but that's why we need to distinguish ourselves. We're all a little different, but our focus is 100 percent coffee."

Meanwhile Jeschke, Lowe and their team continues to make the world a better place through coffee, whether across the globe or across town, one delicious cup at a time.

La Finca Coffee

It's easy to make yourself at home at La Finca Coffee (137 South Central Avenue). First, the smell of freshly roasted coffee draws you in as soon as you walk through the door. Then you hear Latin music softly playing in the background. A cozy sitting area featuring a couch that looks out to the streetscape waits for you to settle in with a cup of coffee. And this is exactly what owners John and Alejandra Hagedorn want.

La Finca, which is Spanish for "small farm," is about thirty miles southwest of downtown St. Louis in Eureka, Missouri. This adventurous young couple opened the business in 2018. John Hagedorn grew up in St. Louis. His mother, a first-generation Mexican immigrant, owned a restaurant in south St. Louis for about ten years, and he helped with the family's business.

Alejandra Hagedorn grew up in Bucaramanga, Colombia. Her father, a professional artist, introduced her to art when she was about seven years old. She went on to help her father in his studio, eventually earned a fine arts degree and immigrated to the United States. While working in childcare in St. Louis, she met John.

While seeing family in Colombia, the couple visited a coffee shop / art gallery owned by a friend of Alejandra's father. "She grew up going to that place," Hagedorn said. He recalled that it was rustic, with stone walls

Alejandra and John Hagedorn, owners of La Finca Coffee in Eureka. *Deborah Reinhardt.*

covered in local artwork. The couple left with an idea to introduce St. Louis to its first Colombian coffee shop.

Jump to early 2018, when Hagedorn's mother, who lived near Eureka at the time, noticed a vacant property on Central Avenue. In several months' time, with no previous experience in coffee or owning a business, but with a lot of sweat equity, they opened La Finca.

Initially, La Finca served coffee roasted by Park Avenue Coffee and later Sump Coffee, and Hagedorn credits respective owners Dale Schotte and Scott Carey for sharing their knowledge with him.

"Then I took it from there," he said. "Getting into the business, I'd developed a relationship with coffee, and that led me to obsessing about it."

Now La Finca's coffee is drum-roasted in-house by Hagedorn. He started with a roaster that could handle one-kilo batches and recently purchased a second ten-kilo roaster. Using Café Imports, Hagedorn started taking beans from Latin American and Ethiopian sources. In time, he grew confident enough to ask reps what was new and in season, get samples to roast and decide whether to add them to his bar. Their website (coffeelafinca.com) lists whole-bean coffee from Brazil, Colombia, Guatemala and Ethiopia. Buena Vibra, a dark roast blend, is recommended for use in cold brews. They also offer an espresso blend.

Hagedorn said that most of their coffees are light or medium roasts, and he takes careful notes regarding time and temperature to ensure consistent quality. He said he'll roast three or four times per week, producing about 80 kilos (about 176 pounds) per day. Some of their specialty drinks on the bar include Tinto (Colombian-style coffee made with sugar) and Café de Olla (Mexican-style coffee with sugar and cinnamon). When these were sampled, they proved to be delightfully balanced. La Finca Coffee is sold at the shop and at Celebrating Life Cake Boutique on Manchester Road in west St. Louis County. (The boutique supplies La Finca with decorated cookies.) Pastries in the case come from Diana's Bakery, a Mexican bakery located on Cherokee Street in St. Louis City.

Experiencing consistent growth, Hagedorn said 2020—despite the pandemic—was their best year. The couple must be doing something right, because they are getting ready to open a second location in the St. Louis neighborhood known as The Grove.

"It just kind of happened," Hagedorn said. "I wanted a place in the city to go back to where I came from." The new location, which is due to open in September 2022, will be at 4440 Manchester Avenue, he said, and will feature a more modern vibe while keeping true to their Latin American heritage. Like the Eureka location, the space will feature Alejandra's art. And the new location will have a kitchen, so Hagedorn said they hope to include house-made Mexican sandwiches.

Hagedorn said La Finca has a few wholesale accounts, but he'd eventually like to see the roastery do a fifty-fifty retail and wholesale split. "We're nearly there now," he added.

After receiving a wish for continued success, Hagedorn responded with a thank-you and chuckled. "You know, I can bury my head in numbers and analysis, but sometimes you just got to do it," he said. "And I learn by doing."

Living Room Coffee & Kitchen

An older woman with cropped white hair emerges from a sporty electric car. As she makes her way into Living Room Coffee & Kitchen (2810 Sutton Boulevard), she passes a young woman with dark hair wearing a face mask holding a to-go cup and a brown paper bag. Both women pass by two female friends on the café's patio, each with a cup of coffee and locked in conversation. Just a typical weekday morning here, where the slogan "all are welcome" is more than a tagline. No matter one's age, status, gender or anything else, it's easy to feel at home at the Living Room.

Owner Nate Larson said his coffee journey took place by happenstance.

After graduating college, Larson worked for an arts center that served people with disabilities. Next to the art studio was a space his father, Barry,

Nate Larson, owner of Living Room Coffee & Kitchen in Maplewood, stands at the coffee roaster. *Deborah Reinhardt.*

rented to roast his own coffee. After several years at the arts center, an "unexpected career change" befell Larson, and while he was between jobs, he and a friend started selling his dad's coffee at farmers markets and developed a successful cold brew.

In 2014, Larson and his buddy opened their café in a space shared with a local whole animal butcher, Bolyard's. Living Room had a few tables that were always full. Larson said his friend handled the coffee and he taught himself to bake and took care of the kitchen. A peanut-butter-and-chocolate-chip cookie was the first thing Larson learned to bake for the café. This gluten-free treat is still popular with his customers.

"Things developed organically from there," he said, adding that the friend has moved on and his sister, Hannah Larson, became a co-owner about a year after the opening. His father, Larson said, is "a silent partner."

Bolyard's relocated to another location on Sutton Boulevard, enabling Living Room to expand its dining room, which was completed in early 2022.

Larson said he gets the green coffee through Café Imports, which vets the global farms that provide the coffee. Depending on the season, Living Room roasts beans from countries including Costa Rica, Ethiopia and Nicaragua. He'll roast up to ten thousand pounds per year, most of it for the retail side, although a small percentage of business is wholesale. The beverage menu is extensive. There's the variety of espresso and specialty lattes (hot or iced), plus tea and hot chocolate. Want a specialty espresso like "sproda" (espresso and root beer)? No problem.

"People ask all the time, 'What's new on the bar?'" Larson said, adding that his customers' knowledge about coffee has come a long way since they've opened, indicative of what's happening around coffee in St. Louis.

The provisions section of Living Room's menu, which was insanely popular at the height of COVID, was kept, because customers grew to love Larson's bread, house-made yogurt and granola. Interestingly, Larson said Living Room Coffee & Kitchen didn't shut down a single day during the pandemic. He had to close the dining room for a time per St. Louis County health protocols, but people ordered online (livingroomstl.com), and staff delivered curbside.

When asked how Maplewood can support several coffee roasters and shops within a small geographic area, Larson said the diversity of offerings lends to the success. "Each shop is totally different," he said. "Foundation Grounds [Maplewood Deli & Coffeehouse] is good if you want to grab a cup of coffee and or work with your laptop. We're a family friendly restaurant. People eat here several times a week or come to share a meal with friends."

NORTHWEST COFFEE ROASTING COMPANY

"I've always been an entrepreneur," said Jason Wilson, owner of Northwest Coffee. Like many entrepreneurs, Wilson knows it's important to keep one eye on the future, to think "what's next" so that business keeps growing or to know when to make timely shifts.

For Wilson, a pivotal shift in his career started his journey into coffee. "I was in the inventory fleet cleaning business," he said. "I was essentially cleaning thousands of vehicles a week for dealerships and large companies that owned a fleet of vehicles."

During this time, Wilson said he started drinking coffee ("I was around thirty-two or thirty-three."). When he needed a break from the office, he'd escape to Starbucks for the Wi-Fi and a cup of coffee. While studying market and economic trends that affected the auto industry, Wilson started thinking what he would do next should the economy take a hit. How would his business be affected?

He was also doing more research about coffee, studying pricing history, consumption trends and why Black people weren't more involved in the industry. After all, coffee's story began in Africa. "[Black] lineage is directly connected to coffee," Wilson said. "I wanted to connect the dots."

By 2006, Wilson had seen enough evidence to know it was time to get out

Breakfast at Northwest Coffee Roasting Company can include a bagel and lox sandwich with a cup of House Blend, a mild combination of Central and South American coffees. *Deborah Reinhardt.*

of the vehicle-cleaning business, so he sold his company and enrolled in business school at Washington University in St. Louis. "When I graduated in 2010, I focused on learning more about coffee," he said. "It [coffee] seemed to be bulletproof, so I put a business model and financing together." In 2012, Wilson bought Northwest Coffee (4251 Laclede Avenue, northwestcoffee. com) from Rick Milton, who opened the business in 1993 but decided it was time for him to sell.

A few months later, Wilson opened Chronicle Coffee, a community-focused coffee café, on the north side of St. Louis in the former Blumeyer public housing complex. Northwest Coffee was served, a space was created for neighbors to gather and he hired young people from the neighborhood. Chronicle Coffee was in business for two years.

When asked what he learned from the experience, Wilson said research sometimes isn't enough. And when Michael Brown, an unarmed Black youth, was shot and killed by Ferguson police officer Darren Wilson in August 2014, the city's tenuous race relations were stretched taught, often to breaking. Coffee was not in the front of Black minds, and many whites were reluctant to travel into Black communities.

"What people say and their actions are different. I couldn't survive there, although people said they wanted a coffee shop, it wasn't enough. You got to have a stronger middle class of folk with discretionary income and with the privilege of having down time."

But Wilson invested his energy into Northwest Coffee, defying odds as a Black person owning a successful coffee roasting and café business. He said showcasing African-grown coffees is important to him. "I like to experiment with them. And when it comes to the coffee trade, to me, they [African coffees] don't get the love they deserve," Wilson said. Coffee from Colombia and Guatemala are also featured. The best-selling house blend is a combination of Central and South American coffees.

His coffee is roasted at lower temperatures for longer periods of time in a 1957 Probat coffee roaster. Wilson said this method allows sweeter notes to come through the beans. "From my perspective, it's similar to when you're baking something. You bake at lower temperatures so the inside bakes first and not the outside," he said. "You're not going to notice it as much in some of the coffees, but you will in the Sumatra because it's less oily and bright."

Using a vintage roaster is old school, but Wilson likes the low-tech approach to coffee. "Sure, you have a model when you go in, but you have to feel it and have a tangible relationship with it. Nothing takes the place of the human element when you create."

During COVID's early months, Wilson remained open and was able to serve customers inside and on the spacious, friendly patio. A former auto garage, the café has a trendy, industrial feel, yet the space is welcoming. In 2021, Wilson enclosed a part of the patio to provide customers with a great indoor space that still connects with the Central West End neighborhood; not unlike having a screened porch on a house. The café also offers a selection of smoothies, tea, hot chocolate and a limited breakfast and lunch menu.

Wilson also collaborated in 2021 with NBA legend Dikembe Mutombo. Northwest Coffee roasts one of the house blends for Mutombo Coffee. The basketball great visited Wilson and Northwest Coffee to have a public conversation about the African coffee industry, particularly in Mutombo's native Democratic Republic of the Congo.

In the spring of 2022, Northwest Coffee opened another location. The café is inside the Schnucks market on Big Bend Boulevard in Webster Groves, not far from Hixson Middle School, which Wilson attended. He often sees old friends come into the new café, and that's a good feeling. The supermarket chain added bags of Northwest Coffee to select stores, further expanding the business's wholesale coffee trade. Wilson said he wants to open more coffee shops within a year, although "nothing is written in stone."

Wilson has adopted "control the narrative" as his company's slogan and business adage. In 2020, he produced *Entrepreneur: St. Louis Edition*, a video by David Kirkman (Woke Nation Entertainment) showcasing several Black businesses. He knows he's breaking down ethnic barriers in the coffee industry and had mixed emotions when Northwest Coffee saw an uptick following the "support Black businesses" movement following the murder of George Floyd.

"It made me feel like, 'Damn, I've been around for a while,' and it irked me a little bit, but at the end of the day, not so much. We're winning on our product being quality and tasting great. That's the win. All these things take time to realize," Wilson said.

PARK AVENUE COFFEE

When asked what led him to the coffee industry, Dale Schotte chuckled and said, "I had no interest in getting in the roasting business," and then the founder and CEO of Park Avenue Coffee added that he doubts anybody graduates school with a plan to open a coffee shop or roasting facility.

Like so many other specialty roasters, Schotte was brought to coffee through a series of life events. About twenty years ago, Schotte—who describes himself as "a huge coffee snob" back then—met a woman at a gym. They struck up a conversation, and he learned that she was working at opening a coffee shop. She discovered that Schotte was an IT specialist. She hired him to assist with getting the network and point-of-sale systems going.

Later, she asked if he could help her with other aspects of the business, which required Schotte to call on his sister, Marilyn Scull, for her expertise in food service. All the while, Schotte found the work interesting and told the shop's owner at her grand opening that if she ever decided to sell, to give him a call.

Less than three years later, that's what happened. But his IT career was going swimmingly. Schotte worked remotely for an out-of-state company and conducted a successful consulting business on the side. Although he told the woman he'd think about it and call her back, he said his intention was to decline the offer—until his sister called.

Unhappy with her longtime employer, Scull had just quit her job in food service and called her brother. The siblings talked, and he shared the news about the offer to buy a coffee shop. The two crunched the numbers and, after discussions, decided to buy it with the idea that it would pay Scull her salary while Schotte kept his IT jobs.

Park Avenue Coffee opened in Lafayette Square, a historical neighborhood near downtown St. Louis, in 2006. "We changed the name, kept consistent hours, and it got busy really quick," Schotte said. "I'd come in at 5:30 a.m. to open and stay until 9:00 a.m., go do my IT jobs. Marilyn worked from noon to 8:00 p.m." Adding a couple of part-time people also helped them out.

But after six months, Schotte realized that something had to give. The hours were too much, so in 2007, he left the IT employer, kept his consulting business and continued helping at the coffee shop. Three years later, he was full-time at Park Avenue.

Today, Park Avenue (parkavenuecoffee.com) has six locations, including the café and roasting facility (5105 Columbia Avenue) that is part of St. Louis's historic Italian neighborhood known as "The Hill." When they opened here in 2012, Park Avenue started to roast its own coffees.

"One of the things important to us was sustainability," Schotte said. "We researched everything we could find and found out air roasting to be much more ecofriendly."

Air-roasted coffee is tumbled on a fluid bed of hot air instead of the traditional steel drum. The air flow is controlled to result in an even roast, and the chaff (the beans' "skin" that falls off during the roasting process) is separated, preventing that material from smoking during the roast.

Their Loring coffee roasters are 90 percent more efficient than traditional drum roasters, Schotte said. The first machine they purchased roasts about thirty pounds at a time; a second machine can do eighty pounds per batch. Schotte said a third roaster is on order. In addition to using much less natural gas to roast their coffee, he said they have solar panels on the roof of their facility. "We are the most ecofriendly roaster in the Midwest," Schotte said.

Sustainability also is evident in how Park Avenue sources its coffee beans. Schotte said they trade directly with farms in Colombia, Costa Rica, Guatemala and Sumatra. "We've been to these farms. We know they're taking care of their staff and their land," he said. Schotte said their espresso is the best seller, and among the seventeen varieties of single-origin or blended drip coffees, the most popular are their Amp'd Blend (dark roast) and the St. Louis Blend (medium roast).

Park Avenue roasts up to 150,000 pounds of coffee per year, Schotte said, with about 20 percent going into their café locations and the rest sold wholesale to a variety of companies in ten midwestern states. They employ fewer than forty people.

Then there are the gooey butter cakes.

Park Avenue's sister baking company, Ann & Allen, is responsible for the seventy-five varieties of a St. Louis favorite, gooey butter cake. Schotte and Scull always served their mother's recipe for the product (although he said they altered the amount of crust) at Park Avenue. But as news of the luscious pastry spread through the region and eventually nationwide, the two realized an expansion was needed. Today, the cakes are shipped around the world, and cake mixes for the traditional, chocolate and white chocolate raspberry flavors were added.

As Schotte and Scull's company continues to spread the coffee and gooey butter love, they're adding a second warehouse and keeping their eyes open for growth opportunities. "I believe opportunities will present themselves. Meanwhile, we're big on doing what we do and trying to do it better than everybody else," he said.

Shaw's Coffee Ltd.

As every medical student will tell you, caffeine is a necessary study aid. While attending medical school in San Francisco, Walter Boyle discovered Peet's Coffee and came to love the rich, dark coffee. So much so that when he moved from California to St. Louis for a job at Washington University in 1987, he brought Peet's Coffee with him.

Boyle and his wife, Gail, own Shaw's Coffee Ltd. (5147 Shaw Avenue). Like most roasters, their path to coffee took the scenic tour.

The couple met while working together at Washington University, where Boyle introduced Gail to Peet's Coffee.

"We had a freezer in our lab that always had ten or twenty pounds of [Peet's] coffee," he said. While working late nights on papers and grants in St. Louis's few coffee shops, Boyle said he found himself missing the West Coast coffee bars even more. Then a call from Boyle's brother in Seattle came; a Probat commercial coffee roaster was for sale. Because friends and family often suggested they roast their own coffee, Boyle said he and Gail bought the roaster and then started to look for a place to roast. After nine months of the roaster in storage, the couple found a space for lease in The Hill neighborhood next door to J. Viviano and Sons Grocers.

"The space needed a little work. It was actually quite a mess; boarded up, full of old Xerox machines," Boyle said. But the price was an offer they couldn't refuse, so they signed the lease and gutted and rehabbed the space. After about eighteen months, Shaw's Coffee had its soft opening in June 1999 as a micro-roastery and café. In 2001, they bought the building, which included a former bank next door, and expanded.

Boyle said their coffees are roasted to the "second crack." Some, especially coffees from Africa, are pulled immediately after, but he said they generally prefer to roast darker. "This is more of a taste decision and something we've just stuck with," Boyle said.

All their coffee is sourced from farms around the world through an importer. "Organic and fair-trade coffees are in the mix for us," he said. Shaw's Coffee buys mountain-grown Arabica coffees from Africa, the Americas and the Pacific Rim, according to Boyle.

Yes, the coffee is still roasted in the machines the couple bought years ago. Boyle said he does the maintenance himself, and after retiring from Washington University (he is a professor emeritus) after thirty-five years, there's more time to tinker. But the area Boyle said he wants to concentrate on is building the online sales for Shaw's Coffee (shawscoffee.com). Single-origin and blends, including the best-selling Italian roast, are available to purchase online and in the shop. Pastries offered at the café are provided through Breadsmith and Companion, two local bakeries.

Although they've talked about opening a second location, Boyle said he and Gail are comfortable on The Hill. You'd have to imagine St. Louis's Italian neighborhood knows a few things about espresso, right?

SUMP COFFEE

It's scary how much Scott Carey knows about coffee. His developed palate could compete with that of any well-trained wine sommelier. In fact, Carey has said that coffee is more chemically complex than wine. In fact, the coffees offered at the bar or online read a little like a wine list: Ethiopia Bensa Segera (notes of berries, ginger and melon); Honduras Yerin (white grape, apple, walnut); and Costa Rica Sabana (apple, strawberry, orange). Packages detail the name of the farm (or even farmer), region grown, altitude and varietal.

Yet even a coffee neophyte would be comfortable at Sump's marvelously cool café (3700 South Jefferson Avenue) inside a three-story building that

Scott Carey opened Sump Coffee on South Jefferson Avenue in 2011. *Courtesy Sump Coffee.*

dates to the 1890s. That's because Carey and his crew do all the heavy lifting for us, so we just get to enjoy a product that many say has reshaped the way St. Louis experiences coffee. Through podcasts and videos (or simply chatting with his customers), Carey shares a great deal of his knowledge and methods using an approachable, soft-spoken demeanor and his ability to boil the science down for the rest of us. If you want to know how post-harvest processing of coffee cherries can heighten or tweak the beans' flavor notes, he's got you covered. Just want an amazing cup of coffee to go? Carey's here for you, too.

Carey, who grew up in St. Peters, Missouri, left the area to go to school (chemistry background) and later law school. He worked for a while as an attorney in New York but came back to St. Louis when his brother became ill. He found a spot for the two of them to live near the place his brother was taking his cancer treatments. The ground floor was suited for commercial use, and Carey, who told a local newspaper he missed New York coffee, wanted to create a product and space around it. As a result, Carey and business partner Marlene Yamaguchi opened Sump Coffee in 2011.

Although roasted beans at first were purchased from other sources around the country, Sump started roasting its own beans in 2013. Carey's "peak-to-peak" roasting method involves purchasing seasonal beans as they hit the U.S. market and then roasting each batch as required to achieve an exact flavor profile. Most of the roasts are on the lighter side, but Carey said Sump doesn't have a signature roast, and what's offered at the café is always evolving. What doesn't change is his commitment to craft the best cup of coffee you may ever have.

Carey describes his customers as people who are "curious and intentional about their life choices." For those who don't live nearby but want access to Sump's coffee, Carey offers coffee subscriptions through the website (sumpcoffee.com) and helpful tutorials to brew great coffee at home.

Visiting Music City for a weekend of fun? Carey's got you covered. In 2016, Sump opened a location in Nashville, Tennessee. And about a year ago, Sump collaborated with Songbird (4476 Chouteau Avenue), providing the coffee service to the breakfast and lunch café that features locally sourced ingredients.

St. Louis is a huge coffee city, Carey said, pointing out the number of roasteries in the area and the city's rich coffee history that he said at one time topped seventy-five roasters. "It's a lot bigger than people think [but] like many things in St. Louis, because of the negative stories and being part of the land bridge between the coasts, it is readily overlooked," he said.

Fortunately for us, Carey is always experimenting. After eleven years in the business, Carey said he still is inspired, because coffee is forever changing. "I have been very touched and surprised by the guests we have met over the years or who continually visit us to this day. St. Louis has some really wonderful people, and we have been fortunate to have met them."

THERE ARE OTHER St. Louis coffee shops that roast their own beans. **Berix Coffee** (2201 Lemay Ferry Road, berixcoffee.com) is a Bosnian restaurant and coffee roastery that has been a part of south St. Louis County since the early 2000s. Its coffee service can be enjoyed at the restaurant, and bags are available through the website. And **Hartford** (3974 Hartford Street, hartfordcoffee.com), a neighborhood café, bakery and coffee shop, has been a staple in the Tower Grove neighborhood in south St. Louis since 2004. Their coffee is air-roasted on site.

The St. Louis area also has roasters whose business is strictly wholesale, providing roasted coffee to cafés, restaurants, convenience stores, hospitals, schools and other institutions and sometimes to coffee shops. Here is a selection of wholesale roasters for you to meet, since you've likely already sampled their coffee.

CHAUVIN COFFEE

It's no stretch to say that coffee is in Dave Charleville's blood.

Charleville is vice-president of operations at Chauvin Coffee (310 South Fillmore, Kirkwood) that has roots going back three generations. After "Java Joe" Charleville sold Rose Coffee Company in 1977 to Ronnoco, he—along with wife, Marge, and stepson Jim Brickey—started Chauvin Coffee in 1984 and operated from Miss Hulling's Restaurant at Eleventh and Locust Streets in downtown St. Louis. In the late 1980s, the company was sold to Brickey. David Charleville Sr. bought into the coffee business in 1995 and, in 1997, bought out Brickey, taking full ownership.

While his family has a rich history in the coffee business, Dave Charleville said he never thought he'd get into it. "I went to Jackson, Wyoming, in 1989, working tables and screen-printing T-shirts. Eventually I got a screen-printing business," he said.

Then devastating news came from home. "My dad got diagnosed with cancer, so he and my mom convinced me and my wife to return to St.

Joe Charleville, founder of Chauvin Coffee, started in the coffee business as a teenager when he worked with his stepdad at Rose Coffee Company. *Courtesy Charleville family.*

Louis," Charleville said. In the early 2000s, Charleville started in sales. His father "threw me into the deep end, but it was great. I learned how to roast, fix espresso machines."

Charleville's father died in 2006 (his grandfather passed in 2011), and he said he ran the coffee business for a year. Although he left coffee for a few years after that, he's been at Chauvin since 2013, adding that his brother and roast master Mike "makes all the magic happen with coffee."

Independent coffee shops make up the core of Chauvin's wholesale business, according to Charleville. "The reason for that is in the late 1990s when Starbucks was taking over the universe, a lot of mom-and-pop types thought 'I'm going to open a coffee shop.' Our coffee customers are pretty much in the St. Louis region. MoKaBe's [a coffeehouse on Arsenal Street in south St. Louis] is our longest-standing company," he said.

But working with coffeehouses and restaurants goes back to the days when Charleville's dad was at the company. "My dad became the first authorized dealer for genuine commercial espresso machines in the Midwest. He knew how to sell them, what made great espresso, and developed special blends," he said. It was knowledge, Charleville added, that his father gained from a ten-day European trip in 1973. His father toured different countries to learn everything about espresso.

"Nobody in this area does what we do as far as being able to help [coffeehouses] get set up technically, sell it, train and get them going, and then sell the other items that go with it," Charleville said. In addition to coffee, Chauvin sells syrups, sauces, tea and smoothie mixes.

And if you want to make Chauvin coffee at home, buy it by the bag online (chauvincoffee.com). The website lists other restaurants and coffeehouses that offer their coffee, as well as a list of retail outlets that sell Chauvin.

When asked what's ahead for the company, Charleville replied, "More of the same." It's clear that Charleville and his family know the recipe for a successful coffee business.

Clipper Coffee

The aroma of freshly brewed coffee was undeniable as shoppers rounded a corner inside Fresh Thyme market in Kirkwood. Tom Charleville is the dapper, silver-haired gentleman handing out his coffee samples. He's happy to chat with those sampling his coffee and to share a bit of Clipper's background, but he's mainly tickled to see their reaction of satisfaction.

Charleville, seventy-three, with nearly fifty years of experience in the coffee business, started Clipper Coffee five years ago, but this isn't his first coffee rodeo. He worked with his family, who owned Rose Coffee, and when that was sold, he launched Thomas Coffee Company in the mid-1980s. At Thomas, Charleville sold coffee to a variety of local restaurants and most country clubs. But after twenty-five years helming Thomas Coffee, Charleville suffered a massive stroke and sold the company.

"That's the only reason I sold it, because of the stroke," he said, adding that his doctors gave him a grim prognosis, saying he wouldn't be able to reason or speak again. But Charleville battled back for six years, and when most men would have been happy to retire quietly (and thankfully), he missed the coffee business and wanted back in it.

In a one-man operation, Charleville roasts his coffee—a European-standard blend of Costa Rican, Colombian and Guatemalan beans—in small batches at the Chauvin plant in Kirkwood. "If I have to be in the back packing coffee, they'll roast for me, but they know what I like and I trust them," he said. (His nephew, Mike Charleville, is the roast master at Chauvin.)

Tom Charleville, son of Joe Charleville (Rose and Chauvin coffee companies), launched Thomas Coffee in 1984. He owned it for twenty-five years. His current business venture is Clipper Coffee. *Deborah Reinhardt.*

He said the beans he purchases from farms in Central and South America are pesticide-free and hand-picked. "It takes three thousand hand-picked beans to make one pound of coffee," Charleville said. The beans are grown in shade at 4,500 to 6,000 feet above sea level. He says this quality of "Euro-prep" beans —what Clipper Coffee buys—represents between 1 and 3 percent of what is exported.

The company's logo, a clipper ship, harkens back to the days when these fast-moving vessels carried cargo such as coffee, spices and tea from Central and South America to New Orleans. The cargo was then sent north on the Mississippi River to St. Louis.

Clipper may be the "David" working alongside the "Goliath" wholesale roasters in St. Louis, but Charleville thinks his coffee speaks for itself. A fine cup of coffee at the end of a meal is critical in the restaurant business, he said. "Some of the [coffee brewing machines] in restaurants can cost several thousand dollars; they're like a Ferarri. But like a Ferarri, if you don't put the right fuel [coffee] in it, it's not going to perform," Charleville said. He added that he's speaking to some local restaurants he's done business with in the past and hopes to expand to other Missouri cities, including Kansas City and Springfield, and to Chicago, Illinois.

Currently, Clipper Coffee—ground and whole-bean in regular and naturally steam-decaffeinated) is available through its website (clippercoffee. com). Local markets carrying Clipper Coffee are Fresh Thyme (selected locations), Dierbergs, Schnucks and Straub's.

"I know I'm starting all over, so have to keep focused," Charleville said. "But I've spent more than forty years developing contacts and my palette; that's what I've got going for me."

Dubuque Coffee Company

It's not a name on the tip of every St. Louisan's tongue, but chances are good that many have sampled Dubuque Coffee. Founded in 2015 by longtime Ronnoco Coffee employee Charles Dubuque, the company, located on Hanley Industrial Court, has wholesale accounts in more than twenty states and a solid presence in St. Louis. A glance at its website (dubuquecoffee. com) lists St. Louis hospitals, cultural institutions, schools, restaurants, coffee shops and private clubs among its clients.

In a *St. Louis* magazine article, Dubuque said the quality of equipment, customer service and coffee itself sets his company apart. In 2020, the *St. Louis Business Journal* reported that Dubuque Coffee worked with David Messner (New Legacy Development Partners) to bring back the Old Judge coffee brand. New Legacy bought the historic Old Judge building on Second Street in 2019 and acquired the necessary trademarks.

First Crack Coffee

Brothers Bryndon and Collin Bay could be a small coffee shop's best friend. Since 2018, they've provided a facility (2204 South Vandeventer Avenue) for specialty coffee businesses to roast their coffee, as well as offer classes and café equipment sales, the latter being their initial focus when the business launched in 2013.

Prior to entering the coffee industry, the brothers and their father worked for Mel Bay Music, a sheet music distributor founded by their grandfather in 1947. After 2008, they noticed a definite economic slide in the business, and Collin Bay said he and his brother made lists of other things they were interested in. "Coffee was on both our lists," he said.

Although Mel Bay Music, based in the St. Louis area, survived the recession (it celebrated seventy-five years in 2022) and continues to be run by their father ("He's never going to retire," Collin said), the brothers moved on, putting their distribution knowledge to use in the coffee industry. They sold Proaster specialty coffee roasters, which are made in Korea. For a few years, they traveled around the United States, visiting thousands of coffee shops, realizing that there was strong interest in the roasting process from business owners and baristas. The brothers also became familiar with barriers many cafés experienced regarding roasting their own beans.

Collin Bay (*center*), and his brother, Bryndon (*right*), are the owners of First Crack Coffee. Adam Caples (*left*) is an employee. *Courtesy First Crack Coffee.*

Bay named those hurdles: roasters are expensive; coffee education is "unbelievably expensive"; a lack of space to install a roaster and to store bags of green coffee; and a perceived mysticism surrounding coffee roasting—that it's too hard to learn

"These challenges prompted Bryndon and I to think about how we could get more people roasting, which ultimately led us to open our facilities," Bay said. "By offering access to equipment, free world-class education, space, and demystifying the roasting process, we were able to help get more people into roasting." They also continue to sell Proaster equipment, as well as coffee roasters by Bühler, a company founded in Switzerland in 1860.

One of First Crack's clients is Toasted Coffee House (3015 High Ridge Boulevard) in Jefferson County, just south of St. Louis. Rachel Walter, co-owner, said she and sisters Emily Haskins and Sarah Bommarito opened Toasted Coffee House in 2017, the first to open in the unincorporated community of High Ridge, Missouri. Originally, the sisters wanted a bakery to sell their dad's delicious sourdough bread. "But a store that sells just bread isn't too appealing," she said.

"We heard a lot of 'Do you think that's going to work? Do they even like coffee?'" Walter said. "We're here to help the community and provide a space to gather or do homework."

Walter said First Crack approached them. "Of course, it sounded awesome to be able to roast our own coffee. It would be almost impossible for a new startup coffee shop. They provided the roaster and education, but you have control over your coffee. Everybody that works there is so passionate about making everything regarding roasting accessible."

They roast about ninety pounds of coffee each week, according to Walter, who added that Haskins devises the drink and food menus for breakfast and lunch service. Seasonal drinks—spring features include a honey lavender latte—are the most popular on the bar, and the bakery's banana bread has been selling like hotcakes.

First Crack recognizes the challenges faced by café owners, and Bay said the backbone of their business is bringing equity to the industry. "The coffee value chain is lopsided," he said. While the industry has highlighted struggles of the small producer, there hasn't been meaningful change "upstream."

"On the other end, we've done a poor job of highlighting the inequity at the downstream end of the value chain. Historically, margins have been large in the middle and have been protected by shrouding roasting in complexity and by having prohibitively expensive education and equipment," Bay said.

Many cafés purchase coffee from roasters who source inefficiently, "spending too much on shipping coffee" and then dealing with high markups, sometimes 300 percent.

To combat these trends, First Crack advocates smart sourcing and logistics, providing access to equipment and providing affordable education. For existing customers, First Crack offers a free sixteen-hour class, "Bean to Brew," that goes over the practical skills (green bean grading, sample roasting, cupping, brewing). "Upon completion, students are able to begin their roasting program in earnest," Bay said.

And it's a successful business model that's working; First Crack (firstcrack. com) also has locations in Kansas City, Missouri; Cleveland, Ohio; and Denver, Colorado. Bay said they plan to expand into other markets.

Meanwhile, interest in First Crack's services remains strong in St. Louis. Bay said they've received inquiries from businesses in Ferguson and Florissant, two north St. Louis County municipalities, areas underserved in terms of coffee stops. But Bay sees St. Louis as a strong coffee market. "I would rate St. Louis's coffee scene among my favorites, if not my favorite. It's criminally underrated and off the radar," he said.

Mississippi Mud Coffee

Mississippi Mud Coffee embodies the phrase "small but mighty." A wholesale and retail coffee producer in the St. Louis suburb of Maplewood, Mississippi Mud knows attention to detail can make all the difference. With just four employees, the company roasts and quickly ships orders with a handwritten note on each bag.

"We don't stock roasted coffee at all," said CEO Chandler Branch. "It's all roasted on demand."

Mississippi Mud Coffee was founded in 2004 by Chris Ruess (who remains with the company) in the Soulard neighborhood. With a background in graphic design and architecture, Ruess felt it made sense to offer his coffee at the Catalyst Coffee Bar inside the Art Saint Louis Gallery on Pine Street, which was the only retail location for Misisippi Mud at the time.

Branch, whose background is in arts administration, relocated from Chicago with his wife (a native St. Louisan) and ran Art Saint Louis for eight years. That's how he met Ruess. Two years ago, he asked Branch if he'd be interested in working for Mississippi Mud.

Mississippi Mud's organic, carbon-neutral-roasted coffee is available through Walmart and some Dierbergs Market locations. Coffee lovers can also order online through Amazon and the company's website (mississippimudcoffee.com).

Branch said other area businesses serve their coffee, including On the Run stores. He also named Avenue Restaurant in Clayton and Sacred Grounds Café and Coffee in Edwardsville, Illinois, among their buyers.

Working with reputable importers who source high-quality beans and pay farmers fair wages, Mississippi Mud sources beans from countries including Brazil, Guatemala, Ethiopia and Colombia. Single-origin and blends are available. He said American-made, computer-assisted roasting machinery is used. Usually, the coffee is roasted in small batches weighing less than thirty pounds at a time.

The impact of COVID in 2020 and early 2021 was "fairly pronounced" for Mississippi Mud Coffee, although grocery store sales went up significantly, Branch said. Some of their coffee shop customers had to shut down for a while. But overall, St. Louis's coffee culture has come through that fire, and the industry is looking good.

"There certainly are outstanding coffee shops and other roasters doing fantastic work," he said. "If you want to explore coffee in this area, you won't run out of offerings."

RECONSTRUCTION COFFEE ROASTERS

A rooster crows from his yard a few houses away from Reconstruction Coffee Roasters. This and the country lane not much wider than my driveway leading to this roastery in Villa Ridge, Missouri, indicate that I am off St. Louis's beaten coffee path. The unincorporated community (population 2,600) in Franklin County is a forty-five-minute drive west of downtown St. Louis via Interstate 44, state Highway 100, and state Route M. However, this newer small-batch roastery has big plans for providing Franklin and St. Louis Counties with excellent specialty coffees.

Reconstruction Coffee in Villa Ridge offers tastings and tours to the public. *Deborah Reinhardt.*

Clayton and Erin Smith and Emily Kappesser (Clayton's sister) opened Reconstruction Coffee (419 Olive Street) in 2020. Clayton and Emily grew up in Villa Ridge, and Erin's grandparents lived in St. Louis. Like most folks in the coffee business, their paths to opening a roastery were not direct ones. Clayton is a teacher and Erin is a professional singer and dancer. Emily owns her own photography/videography business.

But the couple was bitten by the coffee bug and moved from Chicago to Villa Ridge. Clayton and Emily's parents own the property that's home to the roastery, so in 2019, work began on the building that once was a church dating to 1871. Kappesser said most of the building had to be gutted, but some detail was preserved, including the church's cornerstone that's set now on the front of the building. A restored light from the church shines brightly on the front porch.

The threesome successfully launched their coffee roastery after training through Mill City Roasters (manufacturers of gas drum roasting machines), hands-on experimentation and a lot of sweat equity. But as Kappesser explains, all the founding partners were still working at their full-time jobs while starting the roastery. She said her brother was commuting back and forth between Villa Ridge and Chicago.

So, in 2022, the Smiths decided to return to Chicago, but a new owner—Deb Giffin—was brought on board, as was a new master roaster, Nickie Browne. Cofounder Kappesser remained as operations and accounts manager. "I didn't want the doors to close [on Reconstruction], so we approached Deb; she was one of our first customers," Kappesser said.

Giffin has several businesses in the county, including the Swallow's Nest Boutique and Café in nearby Washington, Missouri. Kappesser said Griffin uses Reconstruction Coffee to make the café's cold brew.

Browne has a background in restaurants and wine, brewing and distilling. She said that during the pandemic, she stayed at home to school her five children. "But I've always looked for new opportunities that fit my résumé. This [the coffee roaster position] was perfect timing," said Browne, who was trained by Kappesser's brother and took classes at First Crack Coffee in St. Louis. "It's been a really fun journey, and I'm so excited to start doing my own blends."

Regarding the new owner at Reconstruction Coffee, Browne said that Giffin is "definitely somebody who's willing to do whatever it takes."

Reconstruction's green coffee is sourced through Café Imports. Kappesser said the importer has been wonderful to work with. Reconstruction's website lists single-origin coffees sold as coming from Colombia and Guatemala. For their Signalman blend (one of the top three sellers and a nod to the railroad history of Villa Ridge)—a dark roast with notes of caramel, toffee and wood smoke—beans from Colombia and Ethiopia are used. Their flagship brand, Proclamation, is a medium-roast blend using beans from Ethiopia and Mexico that produces hints of lemon, pecan and molasses. For the women behind Reconstruction Coffee, how the beans are sourced is as important as how it will taste in the end.

"One of our primary concerns was to see the coffee farmers were being given a fair price and the coffee was ethically sourced. As a small-batch roaster, we prefer to work with farms that are two acres in size or less," Kappesser said. They started with a one-kilo roaster but have upgraded to a ten-kilo model.

Reconstruction Coffee sells its products through its website (reconstructioncoffee.com) and ships directly to home. Folks who live in Franklin County can order and pick up using a locker system on the roastery's front porch: pay for the order in advance and pick up using a simple but secure locker system. And for any coffee lover who wants to go a little deeper into Reconstruction Coffee, they offer a Taste and Tour experience that provides a relaxed morning of tasting coffee, learning how it's made and leaving with a bag of coffee for home.

In St. Louis, Reconstruction Coffee is available at the Annex—a delightful combination of deli, bakery and market—in the suburb of Webster Groves. And the company has an interesting collaboration with Honeymoon Chocolates, a bean-to-bar chocolatier in Clayton, another St. Louis suburb.

Kappesser said account development and collaborative partnerships will be her focus now that all the pieces are in place with the new team. And as the distinctive smokestack on Reconstruction's logo indicates, it's full steam ahead for this coffee company that's owned, managed and crafted by women.

RONNOCO

Ronnoco has been a part of St. Louis for more than one hundred years, founded by the O'Connor brothers and then purchased by the Guyol family in the early 1900s. For years, the roastery was on Dodier Street but moved at the outset of its second century to Sarpy Avenue and later to a central location on Boyle Avenue just off Interstate 64/40. Frank Guyol Jr., with more than fifty years in the coffee business, remained involved, although his son Frank Guyol III, vice-president, was running the operations along with William Guyol, Frank Jr.'s younger brother.

In the 1990s, Ronnoco capitalized on the growing convenience store market and expanded the company's reach in the Midwest. By 2012, Ronnocco had 180 employees. In August of that year, Ronnocco sold to Huron Capital Partners, a Detroit-based private equity firm. A historic era for St. Louis coffee was ending, finalized in 2015 with the passing of Frank Jr., who—like Chauvin's Joseph Charleville—was one of the city's last legendary coffee men.

Since 2013, the company—known now as Ronnoco Beverage Solutions—has purchased five companies and grown its footprint to more than forty states. In 2018, Terry McDaniel was hired as CEO, succeeding Scott Meader, who had been at that post since 2013. Today, in addition to coffee, Ronnoco offers clients products such as sweet and flavored iced tea, lemonade, cappuccino and hot chocolate.

THOMAS COFFEE

The Charleville family's coffee tree has several branches, but the roots are deep, and the tradition simply points to making the best coffee they can. In 1984, when his father was launching Chauvin, Tom Charleville started Thomas Coffee. He told *Sauce* magazine at the time that people thought he was "nuts." Charleville said in 2019, "My roots are in coffee," and he decided while making a batch of doughnuts at Donut Drive-In on Chippewa and Watson, which he owned at the time, to return to those roots.

"I was the first in over fifty years to start a new coffee company in the United States," Charleville said in the article. (Well, the first alongside his father at Chauvin.) Whether first or not, it was true that coffee start-ups were risky business; American consumption was down, thanks in part to the rise of soft drinks and the decline of coffee quality.

Charleville wanted to focus on providing quality coffee to restaurants, country clubs and hotels. Thomas Coffee was served at Union Station, the Adams Mark Hotel, Schneithorst's, Bellerieve Country Club, even Uncle Bill's Pancake House, to name a few. "Garavelli's Cafeteria was our first customer," Charleville said. A motorcycle enthusiast, Charleville said Thomas did Biker's Brew coffee for Harley-Davidson Motor Company, a deal that was struck after bumping into Willie G. Davidson, who then was a senior vice-president, during a Sturgis rally.

But in 2007, Charleville suffered a massive stroke; Thomas Coffee was for sale. In 2009, a group of investors bought Thomas Coffee. New CEO Bob Betz was ready to turn the company around. With just ten employees, Betz called on accounts himself. Old equipment was fixed, and original recipes were resurrected. In 2010, he roasted half a million pounds of coffee. Good news was shared at the directors' meeting in June 2011, but that was interrupted by a fire that started in the roaster. The roaster was finished and the building heavily damaged.

Betz called the Charleville family at Chauvin and the Guyol family, which stilled owned Ronnoco at the time. He asked if they could roast beans for Thomas Coffee to meet its contracts, which included St. Louis's major grocery chains. Although both agreed to help, Betz found a roaster in Texas to use until Thomas could reopen.

Jim Covington, president and CEO of Thomas, has led the company since 2012. Beans used by Thomas are sourced through Hacienda La Minta, which owns a coffee estate in central Costa Rica and imports coffees from around the world. Thomas Coffee (thomascoffee.com) is located at 922 South Boyle Avenue.

TOP OFF YOUR CUP: CUPPING AND TOUR AT KALDI'S COFFEE

On entering the offices and roasting facility at Kaldi's Coffee (3983 Gratiot Street), the aroma of roasted coffee greets you, followed by a friendly receptionist who asks you to sign the visitors' log. A small group of coffee lovers—myself and my daughter included—are here for a free tour and coffee cupping. We're lucky to have Bud Patterson, production manager and head roaster, as our host for the hour-plus experience.

The cupping room resembles a lab, but the specimens today are some of the best coffees from around the world. Just three weeks earlier, Kaldi's relaunched the popular free tours and cuppings, which were paused due to the pandemic. Walking through the cupping room door, we face the roastery that has vintage commercial coffee roasters, including a rare seventy-five-kilo Probat machine from 1937. And that's not the oldest they have, Patterson said.

Six coffees are displayed on the table in the cupping room, far less than the roasters typically cup and score. "We do cuppings at least two times a day," Patterson said, adding that thirty to fifty cups—representing one cup per coffee—are laid out on the busiest days.

The roasters also do cuppings for purchasing reasons. "We score these

Top: Bud Patterson, head roaster and production manager for Kaldi's Coffee Roasting Company, leads a cupping class at their roastery on Gratiot Street. *Deborah Reinhardt.*

Bottom: During the cuppings, held each Friday afternoon at Kadi's Coffee Roasting Company, participants see the crust that forms on the cups' tops as part of the brewing process. The roasters break the crust with a clean spoon to savor the coffee's aroma prior to tasting. *Deborah Reinhardt.*

coffees and provide feedback to farmers," Patterson said. "We'll get 2,500 samples per year and purchase up to 200 a year."

Behind us is a scoring sheet written on the glass window. He explains that this was from last week's cupping of freshly harvested samples. To be a "specialty coffee"—representing just 5 to 10 percent of the global coffee market—Patterson said the Specialty Coffee Association (SCA) requires a score of seventy-nine or above on its global scale. One of the scores on the wall was eighty-nine, but none were below eighty-four.

"We're working from a small pool of coffee that's out there. Truth be told, in America, we buy a lot of that coffee. We're the largest consumers of specialty coffee," Patterson said.

As he continues his informative presentation, Patterson demonstrates the full-immersion method of brewing coffee: He's going in without a filter. The chemical reaction of hot water to the roasted, ground coffee creates a "crust." He later demonstrates how to break it to experience the coffee's full aroma. "Basically, I'm popping a bubble of aroma that'll come to my nose," he said.

He skims any oil on the surface off the cups that a filter would have done at home. Now, we're ready to taste. We're each given a spoon, we dip it in a glass of water, scoop a spoonful of the brewed coffee and transfer it to another cup. We bring the cup to our lips and slurp. The process is repeated as we make our way around the table twice. As we taste the tepid coffees, Patterson asks us to identify some of the flavor notes. Even to my unrefined palate, I can pick out some of them.

After the cupping, Patterson, who started at Kaldi's as a teenager, shows us the training area where some of us sample a nitro cold brew, the roasting area and the warehouse. Skids of coffee have been packed up and are ready to ship out.

I leave with a deeper understanding of not only the neighborhood Kaldi's coffee shop I've been familiar with and visited for years, but also with a better appreciation of the entire coffee production chain, from farm to bag. It's a fascinating process that will help me to enjoy my morning cup of joe even more.

Kaldi's offers the free cupping and tour experience every Friday at 2:00 p.m. Advance registration is required. For more information, visit kaldiscoffee.com/pages/cupping.

8

HOME ROASTING
AND BREWING TIPS

While sitting in the culinary classroom at Kirkwood High School, some of us were having flashbacks to our high school home economics classes (not all of them pleasant, by the way). Others shared what prompted them to take this "roast your own coffee" class offered through St. Louis Community College. All of us loved coffee and were curious as to what instructor Roy Lenox had in store for the evening. Could we learn to successfully roast coffee at home? By the end of the class, we'd realize the answer would be—absolutely.

Lenox, an obvious coffee enthusiast, said he started drinking coffee in college "out of necessity." His journey to home roasting began over twenty years ago. "A teammate of mine and I really liked good coffee, so we decided to make our own at work instead of consuming the coffee in the break room," he said. "The first week we each brought in a coffee and on Friday we brewed and compared them to see which coffee we liked better. That coffee we kept until the next week, and the one who had brought the second-best coffee had to purchase another contender for the following week."

The friendly competition continued to improve the coffee quality, eventually leading Lenox to freshly roasted coffee available to purchase online that was shipped immediately to the buyer. "That was way better than what we could find in the grocery stores. That became our standard coffee," he said.

Several years later, Lenox found green (unroasted) coffee online, and he had to try it. He bought a bag and roasted the beans using a West Bend

Poppery hot-air popcorn maker. "From then on, I was hooked. There was no comparison between what I could roast and the commercially available coffee at my local supermarket, and it was much less expensive than having roasted coffee shipped to me," he said.

Why go through the trouble of roasting coffee at home? One word: chemistry. According to Lenox, once roasted, coffee starts oxidizing and can lose half its aroma and flavor in as soon as two weeks. He contends there's a "subculture" within St. Louis of avid home coffee roasters. "Coffee you roast at home is definitely better than any coffee you can purchase," he said.

For the class, we were divided into two- or three-person teams and led to a stove and Whirley-Pop stovetop popcorn maker. Most of us had never seen (or smelled) green coffee beans before, so Lenox passed around some bags that were about the size of a Nestlé Toll House chocolate chip bag. They smelled a bit like grass. Lenox said these were purchased online from an Oakland, California company called Sweet Marias (sweetmarias.com). He also buys green coffee from Burman Coffee Traders (burmancoffee.com), a business located in Madison, Wisconsin. Caracolillo Coffee Mill (ccmcoffee.com) is known for its Colombian coffee and has good pricing but offers no educational support to the home roaster. The one place you don't want to buy coffee from is Amazon.com. Lenox cautions that home roasters can't tell good coffee by reading online reviews; knowledgeable coffee importers are the best source for green coffee, because their business depends on finding customers great coffee.

Next, Lenox explained that it was important to precisely weigh the green beans, so a digital kitchen scale is helpful to have. He portioned 226 grams, about 8 ounces, for each of us to roast. He turned up the stove's burner, and the popcorn pot was placed on the heat and the beans poured in. The handle on the outside of the pot was attached to the patented stirring mechanism inside, which allowed us to keep the beans constantly moving through the roasting stages. With the popper's lid open, we watched the beans move to the yellow stage (when they start to steam) and then to a cinnamon color. Then, at around 450 degrees Fahrenheit, the first crack occurred. This is followed by what Lenox called a short quiet period, about fifteen or twenty seconds without any "popping" sounds. Lenox said that at this stage, many people prefer to remove the beans from the heat to begin the cooling process. This, he said, allows the coffee drinker to taste the origins of the coffee.

To cool the coffee, the beans were carefully dumped into a fine-grain strainer and shaken gently by hand over a kitchen sink for about ten minutes (or until the coffee cools to one hundred degrees Fahrenheit). During this process, the chaff from roasted beans falls into the sink to be easily rinsed down the drain.

Our finished roasted beans truly smelled divine; we were eager to use them at home.

Darker roasts also are achievable by the home roaster using this method. Lenox said that after the short quiet period passes, the second crack is achieved. For espresso, roast through the second crack until the beans turn a dark, shiny brown. Be warned: this will create a great deal of smoke in your kitchen.

This demonstration proved that by using the most fundamental equipment, one could roast coffee at home. However, it's not the best method if you want consistent results. Lenox shared that green coffee suppliers often sell equipment helpful to the home roaster. Hot-air and drum roasters for home are available; let your budget be your guide. One thing you don't want to skimp on is your coffee grinder, Lenox said. "Your grinder has two jobs—to grind the coffee beans to a various size and to do so as uniformly as possible." The size of coffee granules depends on how long the coffee beans will spend in contact with the water, he added.

"In a French press, the beans sit in the hot water for three or four minutes and if the grounds are too fine, the coffee will taste bitter. While in a standard coffee maker, where the water flows through the grounds in a matter of seconds, using coarsely ground beans would result in weak coffee," said Lenox, adding that conical burr grinders are generally more reliable and give more consistent results than blade grinders or flat burr grinders. He recommends the Capresso Infinity conical burr grinder for less than $100 or the Baratza Encore, a quality grinder that's usually under $170; St. Louis–area shops that sell this grinder are Blueprint Coffee and Reconstruction Coffee.

Emily Kappesser is cofounder and operations manager at Reconstruction Coffee in Villa Ridge, Missouri. A consistent grind for brewing at home is an important detail that's sometimes missed. "I know a lot of people don't realize how important a good coffee grinder is," she said. She said it often takes a few experiments to get the correct setting for the coffee machine you have at home.

Kappesser recommended a simple pour-over method to make a great cup of coffee at home. It's a simple, clean and low-tech way to make coffee. Freshly ground coffee is placed in a cone-shaped ceramic "dripper" with a paper filter. Hot water is poured in a circular motion to wet all the grounds;

pour quickly for a lighter brew, slowly for a richer cup. Reconstruction Coffee sells Hario and Chemex products.

Lenox agrees. "You don't have to spend a lot on coffee makers. That's where people get it wrong," he said. "Great coffee can be made in the morning or any time of day using something as simple as a Melitta or Chemex pour-over filter or a French press. You heat the water to nearly boiling and then pour it over the coffee grounds in the filter or in the French press."

The French (or coffee) press has origins in nineteenth-century France, but a patent for a coffee press similar to those seen today dates to 1929 and Italian designer Attilio Calimani. The modern coffee press uses a metal plunger and mesh filter to press coffee to the bottom of a glass beaker. After the hot water is poured, a lid is placed over the beaker and the coffee steeps for about four minutes. Coffee presses can brew anywhere from one to four cups at a time.

While convenient, the electric, multicup coffee makers don't produce the best tasting coffee. "All those buttons and chrome are dazzling, but most standard coffee makers don't heat up the water enough to extract the full flavor from the coffee bean, a flaw that keeps them from ever making the best coffee," he said.

Lenox said that coffee can be stored in the pantry or on the counter either as whole roasted beans or ground; air-tight glass containers are preferred. But whole beans will stay fresher longer; ground coffee should be used within the week, he said.

Does all of this knowledge to roast and brew coffee at home negate a desire to visit coffee shops? Not at all. Lenox said the St. Louis coffee culture "is pretty good," giving it a seven or eight on a scale of ten. "Unfortunately, much of the volume and profit in St. Louis, like everywhere else, is in the flavored espresso drinks. But there are many good, independent shops that still try to serve just great coffee from all around the world," he said.

9
CONCLUSION

Coffee has had a presence in St. Louis since the city's beginnings, and while there is a strong coffee culture here today, there is room for growth in the metropolitan area, and that's exciting.

As people came through St. Louis on their way west in the mid-nineteenth century, St. Louis grocers and a handful of coffee roasters helped to outfit their wagons. After the Civil War, the number of coffee companies grew to the extent that, by the 1920s, St. Louis was the largest inland coffee roasting hub in the United States.

Over the years, St. Louis's coffee industry has had inventors and big dreamers, all of whom shared a single passion: making the best coffee available to their customers. And while there is a dark part to our coffee history, namely European colonization and the use of enslaved people to farm the beans, many coffee roasteries and cafés in the city either trade directly with farmers or work with importers who ethically source the green beans. In addition, there are some coffee roasteries and shops in the city owned by people of color, and with a need to invest in underserved areas, that number of cafés will continue to grow.

So, the extensive history is being augmented with a robust coffee culture in St. Louis, continuing our story to the present with great possibilities for the future. Just ask some of the folks in town who keep their fingers on the pulse of what St. Louis eats and drinks.

Liz Wolfson is managing editor of *Sauce*, the locally owned, independent monthly magazine that covers St. Louis's culinary scene. Wolfson moved from New Orleans to St. Louis two years ago. Relocating from a great coffee city to another isn't lost on Wolfson, who said she started drinking coffee as a teen. We chatted about the city's coffee scene over cups of java at Coffeestamp. While recognizing the early contributions to the local coffee culture by Kaldi's, she said the city turned a corner when Sump Coffee opened.

"Sump had a clear vision of what coffee should taste like, highlighting all of the nuances of the product," Wolfson said. "That was a big moment."

She lists a few of the independent cafés in town—the Living Room, Coma Coffee, Blueprint Coffee—and notes that St. Louis is in a good place now. "You're not lacking a good, ethically sourced cup of coffee in St. Louis," she said.

And unlike New Orleans—a well-established food city that Wolfson said can sometimes be snobby about its culinary offerings—St. Louisans are open to trying all sorts of food and drink, if it's good.

In February 2022, *Feast*—another magazine covering Missouri's culinary developments—devoted its entire issue to the coffee scene in St. Louis and other cities. In the issue, then editor Heather Riske admitted that at first she was skeptical of the idea. But she wrote, "Would the stories be varied enough to constitute an entire issue? Happily, the answer was a resounding yes."

Collin Bay, co-owner of First Crack Coffee, said coffee consumption has rebounded from the lowest point during the early part of the COVID pandemic, but he thinks the dust needs to settle a bit before predicting if there is room for more shops. "That said, speaking specifically to the St. Louis market, there's a ton of room for growth," Bay added. "I see growth potential all over—urban, suburban and rural St. Louis, but I would draw special attention to north St. Louis City and County. LaJoy's [LaJoy's Coffee Café, 8909 Lackland Road in Overland] is a customer of ours; they're doing a great job.

"By comparison, a city like Seoul [South Korea] has cafés on literally every street corner. Dentists and hair stylists have coffee roasters in their practices. Thirty-three percent of new coffee businesses there fail due to market saturation. We are nowhere near that level of saturation."

Wolfson also hopes to see more coffee shops open in the area. "Every neighborhood should have a coffee shop where you can get a decent cup of coffee and a good pastry. That's the essence of the quality of life. My dream is for every neighborhood to have that," she said.

TOP OFF YOUR CUP: MORE TO EXPLORE

Some coffee drinkers are satisfied to sip in their neighborhood shop, and when we're pressed for a quick cup of java, that's perfectly fine. But there's a plethora of coffee shops in the area, with a good concentration in central and south St. Louis. You might find live music at some of these spots, while others offer cats to cuddle (Mauhaus Cat Café and Lounge, Maplewood).

Neighboring counties that butt up to St. Louis have additional coffee spots you can explore. In St. Charles County, Upshot Coffee roasts for its locations in Cottleville and St. Charles City and for wholesale clients. Course Coffee Roasters on North Second Street in St. Charles, Missouri, includes coffee flights in its espresso bar options, plus a new coffee wine and a coffee mead. Several other options that feature locally roasted coffee are in St. Charles, including Picasso's on North Main Street. And check out St. Charles's impressive lineup of boutiques, antiques stores and restaurants while you sip and stroll.

In Franklin County, Seek Coffee & Cocktails in New Haven, Missouri, combines coffee with cocktails, wine and beer in its tasting room on Maupin Avenue. Tastings are offered on weekends, or you can book a cupping and home brewing class that includes a bag of their roasted coffee. New Haven, also home to Pinckney Bend Distillery, is a sleepy Missouri River town that's close to some of the state's best wineries. Just east of New Haven, Washington, Missouri, is another river town with a handful of coffee stops, including Exit 11 that has two locations on Jefferson Street. The Saturday farmers market is always good, but other attractions, shops and restaurants are there to enjoy.

Drive about thirty minutes south of St. Louis, and you're in Jefferson County, home to several coffee shops. If coffee and ice cream are your favorite things, Pine Mountain Country Coffee on East Main Street in Festus has you covered. Want something more substantial? Try a steamed bagel sandwich for breakfast or lunch. Then shop Main Street or explore a nearby winery or state park. A new coffee roaster, Festus Coffee Company, opened in March 2022. It offers online sales and a retail space at Creations on Main. Their coffee also is sold at Train Town Treasures in De Soto, Missouri, as well as at Makers on Main in Columbia, Illinois. Historic Ste. Genevieve, Missouri, is about forty-five miles south of Festus, if you want to make a full day of exploring. To the north (about fifteen miles) of Festus is the charming Mississippi River town of Kimmswick. You may catch a riverboat in port on your visit.

Across the Mississippi River, Goshen Coffee Roasters has been part of Edwardsville, Illinois, for twenty years. Coffee lovers on both sides of the river can find their brand in local grocery stores, and Goshen also services wholesale clients in St. Louis. In April 2022, Goshen opened its second location in the Soulard neighborhood of St. Louis. Cafés offer a full coffee bar as well as pastries, burritos, toasts with gourmet toppings, salads and bowls. Home to Southern Illinois University–Edwardsville, the city also offers a children's museum, a nature preserve, a restored Federal home open for tours and the Wildey Theater.

In March 2022, *Food & Wine* identified St. Louis as the next great food city. As a result, St. Louis–based food writer Holly Fann wrote an online article for the publication that highlighted some of the city's achievements and anticipated restaurant openings. Although Fann didn't get into coffee for the article, she captured the civic price St. Louis has when it comes to its food and drink, writing, "We are engaged and informed, internalizing an immutable pride, knowing just how outstanding a food city St. Louis is."

St. Louis has been in the national coffee conversation for over 150 years, allowing the craftmanship of its roasters to do most of the talking. But we've known all along that to find a great cup of coffee, we just follow our noses, realizing all the while that we won't have to travel far.

BIBLIOGRAPHY

Chapter 1

Brown, Kathryn Sergeant. "Beavers the Boomtown: Remembering the St. Louis Fur Trade." *Missouri Conservationist* (February 1997).

Chouteau, Auguste. *Fragment of Col. Auguste Chouteau's Narrative of the Settlement of St. Louis.* St. Louis, MO: George Knapp & Company, 1858.

Fatherty, William Barnaby, S.J. *St. Louis: A Concise History.* St. Louis, MO: St. Louis Convention and Visitors Commission, 1990.

McDermott, John F. *Frenchmen and French Ways in the Mississippi Valley,* Edwardsville: Southern Illinois University, 1969.

State Historical Society of Missouri. "The Chouteau Brothers." https:// historicmissourians.shsmo.org.

Toft, Carolyn, ed. *Carondelet: The Ethnic Heritage of an Urban Neighborhood.* St. Louis, MO: Landmarks Association of St. Louis Inc., 1975.

Chapter 2

Holland, Dorothy G. "St. Louis Families from the French West Indies." St. Louis, MO: February 1964.

Pendergrast, Mark. *Uncommon Grounds: The History of Coffee and How It Transformed Our World.* New York: Basic Books, May 1999.

Princeton University Brazil Lab. "Racialized Frontiers: Slaves and Settlers in Modernizing Brazil." https://brazillab.princeton.edu/research/racialized_frontiers.

Stone, Suzanne. *New Orleans Coffee: A Rich History.* Charleston, SC: The History Press, 2019.

Chapter 3

Cultural Resource Management. "Mr. Fuller's Most Peculiar Firearm." Vol. 22, no. 7 (1999).

Edwards, Richard/Hopewell, M. *Great West: A General View of the West and A Complete History of St. Louis.* St. Louis, MO: Edwards Monthly, 1860.

Kargau, Ernst. *Mercantile, Industrial and Professional St. Louis.* St. Louis, MO: Nixon-Jones Printing, 1903.

KWMU 90.7. "If War Is Hell, Then Coffee Has Offered U.S. Soldiers Some Salvation." *Morning Edition*, July 25, 2016.

Leslie, Eliza. *Miss Leslie's Directions for Cookery, in Its Various Branches.* Bedford, MA: Applewood Books, 1853.

Manuel, Jeff. "The National Enameling and Stamping Company." Edwardsville, IL: Madison Historical: Online Encyclopedia and Digital Archive for Madison County, Illinois. July 5, 2017.

Sauce. "Step Aside, Seattle." December 2002.

Simmons Spice Mill. New York: Spice Mill Publishing Company, September 1919.

Stevens, Walter Bartholonew. *Centennial History of Missouri: One Hundred Years in the Union.* St. Louis, MO: S.J. Clark Publishing, 1921.

Ukers, William Harrison. *All About Coffee.* New York: *Tea and Trade Journal*, 1922.

Yearbook of the Commercial, Banking and Manufacturing Interests of St. Louis. St. Louis, MO: S.F. Howe and Company, 1882.

Chapter 4

Greater St. Louis. "St. Louis Ranks as One of the Most Important Coffee Centers in the United States." St. Louis, MO: St. Louis Chamber of Commerce, 1920.

Hahn, Valerie. "World's Fair Plate Tells the Story of a President, a Cabin and a Coffee Company." St. Louis Today, May 19, 2017. www.stltoday.com.

Leonard, John William Leonard, ed. *Who's Who in Finance and Banking*. New York: Joseph & Sefton, 1922.

Loughlin, Caroline/Anderson, Catherine. *Forest Park*. Columbia: University of Missouri Press and the Junior League of St. Louis, 1986.

Memories of the Great St. Louis World's Fair and Scenes from the Most Complete Coffee Plant in the World. St. Louis, MO: C.F. Blanke Tea and Coffee Company, 1904.

Schwendinger, Kristen. "St. Louis's Historic Fix on Coffee." *Gateway* (Fall 2002).

Chapter 5

Corbett, Suzanne, and Deborah Reinhardt. *A Culinary History of Missouri: Foodways & Iconic Dishes of the Show-Me State*. Charleston, SC: The History Press, 2021.

Missouri History Museum. Library Archives. Terminal Railroad Association Records collection.

———. "St. Louis in the Great Depression." July 26, 2017.

Pendergrast, Mark. *Uncommon Grounds: The History of Coffee and How It Transformed Our World*. New York: Basic Books, May 1999.

Quinn, James P. *Scientific Marketing of Coffee*. New York: Tea & Coffee Trade Journal Company, 1960.

St. Louis Globe-Democrat. "City to Observe Second Wartime Thanksgiving." November 21, 1943.

———. "Cup of Coffee Makes or Mars." May 2, 1937.

———. "Soldier Brings Home Bottle of Cooties." May 10, 1919.

———. "Women Must Cook Better to Satisfy Returning Troops, Says Dietician." June 14, 1942.

St. Louis Media History. www.stlmediahistory.org.

St. Louis Post-Dispatch. "Coffee Rationing Ends Due to Rise in Supply; More Sugar Likely Soon." July 29, 1943.

———. "Recipe for Making Coffee Go Farther." Letter to the editor. November 26, 1942.

St. Louis Star and Times. "How to Make Coffee Without a Single Bean." November 5, 1942.

———. "WPA Blamed for Shortage of Coffee." October 27, 1942.

Chapter 6

HEC-TV. "Dana Brown's Life on Safari." December 9, 2010.

New York Times. "Chock Full Corp. Buys 3 Concerns." July 29, 1964.

O'Neil, Tim. "Gaslight Square Burned Bright in the 1960s: What Went Wrong?" St. Louis Today. www.stltoday.com.

Pendergrast, Mark. *Uncommon Grounds: The History of Coffee and How It Transformed Our World*. New York: Basic Books, May 1999.

Quinn, James P. *Scientific Marketing of Coffee*. New York: Tea & Coffee Trade Journal Company, 1960.

Riverfront Times. "The Life and Death of 'Java' Joe Charleville, Local Coffee Icon." April 7, 2011.

St. Louis Globe-Democrat. "Old Judge Food Corp. Sold to New York Firm." June 28, 1957.

St. Louis Post-Dispatch. "Chicago Firm Buys Forbes Coffee Co." February 9, 1956.

———. "James H. Forbes Co. Sold to Toledo Firm." May 3, 1956.

———. "James J. O'Connor Co. Buys Hicks-Jensen Coffee Firm." May 17, 1951.

———. "O'Connor Coffee Acquires Cousins Tea & Coffee." May 24, 1962.

———. "O'Connor Coffee Buys Firm." March 27, 1964.

———. "Ronnoco Coffee Buys Demmas." October 9, 1964.

———. "Ronnoco Coffee Co. Installs New Roaster." March 3, 1969.

———. "Ronnoco Coffee Company's Frank J. Guyol Jr." January 15, 1989.

———. "Vaughan to Retire After 52 Years Behind Counter of His Coffee Store." March 14, 1967.

Chapter 7

Mack, Mary. "With Coffeestamp, Brothers Patrick and Spencer Clapp Offer St. Louisans a Taste of Single-Origin Coffees from Around the World." *Feast* (February 16, 2022).

Sauce. "Step Aside, Seattle." December 2002.

St. Louis Business Journal. "Kaldi's New Owners Hope to Perk $10 Million in Sales." September 16, 2007.

St. Louis Post-Dispatch. "Competitors Show Uncommon Kindness After Misfortune Strikes." September 2, 2011.

INDEX

ABOUT THE AUTHOR

Deborah Reinhardt is a native St. Louisan and an award-winning travel and food writer. She cowrote *A Culinary History of Missouri: Foodways & Iconic Dishes of the Show-Me State* (The History Press, 2021) with Suzanne Corbett. As author of *Delectable Destinations: A Chocolate Lover's Guide to Missouri*, Deborah believes that quality chocolate—and a good cup of coffee—are two of life's greatest pleasures. In 2020, Deborah launched her food blog, ThreeWomenintheKitchen.com, with a focus on comfort food and wisdom from her mother, grandmother and other home cooks; it has received state and national awards. She self-published a family cookbook, *Three Women in the Kitchen: Recipes and Stories of Growing Up in St. Louis*, in 2021 and donated proceeds to Circle of Concern, a food pantry in her area. For more information, follow her on Facebook and Instagram (@threewomeninthekitchen).

She is co-president of Missouri Professional Communicators, the Missouri affiliate of the National Federation of Press Women, as well as a member of the St. Louis Culinary Society. Deborah is a journalism graduate of Southern Illinois University–Edwardsville.

Visit us at
www.historypress.com